Apress Pocket Guides

Apress Pocket Guides present concise summaries of cutting-edge developments and working practices throughout the tech industry. Shorter in length, books in this series aims to deliver quick-to-read guides that are easy to absorb, perfect for the time-poor professional.

This series covers the full spectrum of topics relevant to the modern industry, from security, AI, machine learning, cloud computing, web development, product design, to programming techniques and business topics too.

Typical topics might include:

- A concise guide to a particular topic, method, function or framework

- Professional best practices and industry trends

- A snapshot of a hot or emerging topic

- Industry case studies

- Concise presentations of core concepts suited for students and those interested in entering the tech industry

- Short reference guides outlining 'need-to-know' concepts and practices.

More information about this series at `https://link.springer.com/bookseries/17385`.

Microsoft Dynamics 365 Business Central Essentials

Core Concepts Made Simple

Dr. Gomathi S

Apress®

Microsoft Dynamics 365 Business Central Essentials: Core Concepts Made Simple

Dr. Gomathi S
Chennai, Tamil Nadu, India

ISBN-13 (pbk): 979-8-8688-2228-5   ISBN-13 (electronic): 979-8-8688-2229-2
https://doi.org/10.1007/979-8-8688-2229-2

Managing Director, Apress Media LLC: Welmoed Spahr
Acquisitions Editor: Smriti Srivastava
Editorial Assistant: Jessica Vakili

Cover designed by eStudioCalamar

Distributed to the book trade worldwide by Springer Science+Business Media New York, 1 New York Plaza, New York, NY 10004. Phone 1-800-SPRINGER, fax (201) 348-4505, e-mail orders-ny@springer-sbm.com, or visit www.springeronline.com. Apress Media, LLC is a Delaware LLC and the sole member (owner) is Springer Science + Business Media Finance Inc (SSBM Finance Inc). SSBM Finance Inc is a **Delaware** corporation.

For information on translations, please e-mail booktranslations@springernature.com; for reprint, paperback, or audio rights, please e-mail bookpermissions@springernature.com.

Apress titles may be purchased in bulk for academic, corporate, or promotional use. eBook versions and licenses are also available for most titles. For more information, reference our Print and eBook Bulk Sales web page at http://www.apress.com/bulk-sales.

Any source code or other supplementary material referenced by the author in this book is available to readers on GitHub. For more detailed information, please visit https://www.apress.com/gp/services/source-code.

If disposing of this product, please recycle the paper

Table of Contents

About the Author

 **Dr. Gomathi S** is a Microsoft Most Valuable Professional (MVP), Microsoft Certified Trainer (MCT) Community Lead, and Microsoft Learn Expert with a global footprint in the tech education space. With deep expertise in Dynamics 365 Business Central, Power BI, and AI-powered analytics, she has empowered thousands of learners worldwide through hands-on training sessions, certification programs, and mentorship.

As a passionate professional in training, she is dedicated to bridging the gap between academia and industry, especially through her mission to uplift rural students and educators by equipping them with digital skills and real-world career readiness. Dr. Gomathi is also the creator of the popular YouTube channel Goms Tech Talks, where she shares practical insights on Power BI, Business Central, and other Microsoft technologies through bootcamps, hackathons, tutorials, and expert interviews. Her content has become a valuable resource for students, educators, and professionals seeking to deepen their knowledge.

A global author, speaker, and tech community advocate, Dr. Gomathi is passionate about making technology education inclusive, practical, and impactful.

About the Technical Reviewer

 **Saurav Dhyani** is a Microsoft MVP and founder of Edhate Consulting Private Limited, a company specializing in Microsoft Dynamics 365 Business Central implementation, support, and training. With over a decade of experience in ERP consulting and solution architecture, he has helped organizations worldwide streamline their operations through Business Central. Saurav is also the creator of the popular YouTube channel "Saurav Dhyani," where he shares insights, tutorials, and best practices on Business Central development and administration. Passionate about community learning, he actively contributes through his Teams community, Saurav's Dynamic Hub, and various #BCOpenDiscussion and #BCQuickTip initiatives.

Foreword

By Kennie Nybo Pontoppidan

The way businesses operate is changing faster than ever. Success today isn't just about managing processes; it's about embracing innovation, staying agile, and unlocking insights that drive growth. Microsoft Dynamics 365 Business Central is at the heart of this transformation. It empowers organizations to connect finance, operations, and decision-making in a single, intelligent platform. But with great capability often comes complexity, and that's where clarity becomes essential.

Microsoft D365 Business Central Essentials is more than a guide; it's a catalyst for confidence. In just about 100 pages, this book distils the essence of Business Central into practical, actionable knowledge. It starts with the fundamentals, then moves through functional and technical essentials, and finally offers consultant tips and career guidance. Each chapter is designed to help you not only learn the system but envision how it can shape the future of your business or your career.

What makes this book remarkable is Dr. Gomathi's passion for making Business Central simpler and more useful. That passion translates into a resource that is approachable yet powerful, a quick reference you can rely on when time is short and expectations are high. It's written for learners, consultants, and professionals who want clarity without compromise.

The future belongs to those who adapt, and Business Central is a platform built for that future. This book invites you to explore, to learn, and to lead with confidence. Keep it close, use it often, and let it inspire you to unlock new possibilities.

CHAPTER 1

Business Central in a Nutshell

The first chapter lays the foundation for understanding Microsoft Dynamics 365 Business Central. Before exploring advanced features, customizations, or role-specific processes, it is important to begin with the basics: what the platform is, how it is delivered, who uses it, and how to navigate the interface. By starting here, readers will gain the confidence to move through the application with ease and understand how different roles interact with the system in day-to-day scenarios.

The chapter begins with an overview of Business Central, positioning it as Microsoft's modern ERP solution for small and medium-sized businesses. Readers are introduced to the purpose of the platform and the problems it solves, from managing finance and supply chain operations to handling sales, purchasing, projects, and services. The overview also highlights its seamless integration with Microsoft 365, Power Platform, and the growing role of AI-powered features, showing why BC stands out in today's ERP landscape.

Next, the chapter explains the two primary deployment models: cloud and on-premises. Cloud deployments offer scalability, automatic updates, and reduced infrastructure costs, making them ideal for organizations that

Dr. Gomathi S, *Microsoft Dynamics 365 Business Central Essentials*, Apress Pocket Guides,
https://doi.org/10.1007/979-8-8688-2229-2_1

value agility. On-premises deployments, on the other hand, provide more control and customization but require greater investment in IT resources. By comparing these options, readers can understand the trade-offs and identify which model best fits different organizational needs.

From there, the discussion shifts to roles within Business Central. Readers learn the difference between functional and technical roles. Functional roles include consultants, managers, and end users who rely on the system to perform business operations. Technical roles, such as developers and administrators, are responsible for configuring, extending, and maintaining the system. This section emphasizes how both groups work together to ensure the successful adoption and growth of Business Central within an organization.

Once the context is clear, the chapter turns to navigation tips. Readers are guided through the user interface, exploring features like Role Centers, action bars, search functions, and personalization options. These tips are practical and designed to make readers feel comfortable navigating the system efficiently, saving time and avoiding the frustration that often comes with learning a new ERP.

The chapter concludes with snapshots of the key modules that make up Business Central. Instead of going deep into details, this section gives readers a "tour" of major areas such as Finance, Sales, Purchasing, Inventory, and Projects. These snapshots create a mental map of the system and set the stage for deeper dives in later chapters.

By the end of this chapter, readers will have a clear idea of what Business Central is, the deployment choices available, the roles involved, and how to navigate the system with confidence. They will also carry a high-level understanding of its key modules, preparing them for the more detailed exploration that follows.

Business Central Overview

Microsoft Dynamics 365 Business Central, often called simply *Business Central*, is Microsoft's flagship enterprise resource planning (ERP) solution for small and mid-sized organizations. At its core, Business Central is designed to bring together all the moving parts of a business, finance, sales, supply chain, projects, and services, into a single, connected system. Instead of relying on multiple disconnected applications or manual processes, companies can use Business Central to manage their operations with accuracy, consistency, and efficiency.

Business Central is more than just accounting software. While it does offer strong financial management capabilities, it extends far beyond bookkeeping. A company can track customer orders from quotation to invoicing, monitor inventory levels in real time, streamline purchasing, manage fixed assets, oversee projects, and even support service management. This makes it an "all-in-one" solution where information flows seamlessly across departments, enabling better decision-making.

History and Evolution of Business Central

Business Central did not appear overnight. It has a long history that stretches back more than three decades, starting with a product called **Navision**. Developed in Denmark in the 1980s, Navision was designed as a flexible accounting and ERP solution for small and medium-sized businesses. Its strength lay in its ability to adapt to different industries and countries, quickly gaining popularity across Europe.

In 2002, Microsoft recognized the potential of Navision and acquired it, merging it into the **Microsoft Business Solutions** family alongside other ERP products like Great Plains and Axapta. Navision was rebranded as **Microsoft Dynamics NAV**, and over the years, Microsoft invested heavily in its development. Dynamics NAV became one of the most widely used mid-market ERP systems in the world, known for its powerful customization capabilities and strong partner ecosystem.

For most of its life, Dynamics NAV was an **on-premises solution**, installed on company servers and managed by IT teams. While this gave businesses a high degree of control, it also meant they were responsible for upgrades, hardware, and maintenance. As cloud computing began to reshape the technology landscape, Microsoft realized that ERP needed to evolve in the same direction.

In 2018, Microsoft launched **Dynamics 365 Business Central**, the next chapter in Navision's journey. Business Central took the proven functionality of Dynamics NAV and reimagined it as a modern, cloud-first solution. By delivering it as part of the Dynamics 365 family, Microsoft aligned Business Central with its broader cloud strategy, integrating it closely with Microsoft 365, the Power Platform, and Azure services. The evolution of Business Central across the decades is shown in Figure 1-1.

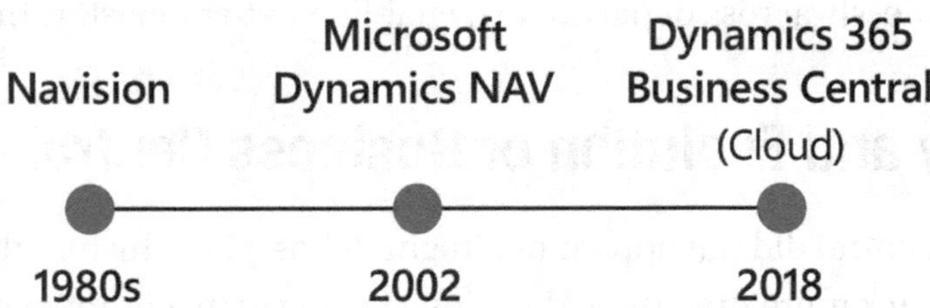

Figure 1-1. *The evolution of Business Central: from Navision in the 1980s, to Microsoft Dynamics NAV in 2002, and finally to Dynamics 365 Business Central (cloud-first) in 2018*

Today, Business Central represents both continuity and innovation. It carries forward the legacy of NAV, trusted, flexible, and rich in functionality, while adding the benefits of cloud delivery: regular updates, scalability, global accessibility, and AI-driven insights. For long-time NAV users, Business Central feels familiar, yet it also opens doors to new possibilities that were not possible in the traditional on-premises world.

Important   Business Central may feel like a "new product," but it's built on decades of reliability from NAV/Navision. This means it combines **proven ERP logic** with **modern cloud innovation**.

This history helps explain why Business Central looks the way it does today. It is not a brand-new product, but the result of decades of refinement, customer feedback, and technological evolution. Understanding this background gives readers confidence: they are working with a system that combines proven reliability with cutting-edge innovation.

Integration with Microsoft Ecosystem

One of the strongest advantages of Business Central is that it is not a stand-alone ERP system. Instead, it is part of the wider Microsoft ecosystem, which means it works seamlessly with the tools that many businesses already use every day. This integration reduces the need for switching between different applications, ensures data consistency, and creates a more connected workplace.

Business Central connects naturally with **Microsoft 365 applications**. For instance, users can create and send sales quotes directly from **Outlook**, turning emails into transactions without leaving the inbox. In **Excel**, financial and operational data from Business Central can be exported, analyzed, and even modified before syncing back into the system. Integration with **Teams** enables employees to collaborate on orders, invoices, or projects by sharing data directly in chats and meetings. These connections bring ERP closer to the day-to-day productivity tools people are already comfortable with.

Beyond Microsoft 365, Business Central is tightly linked with the **Power Platform**. Through **Power BI**, users can build rich dashboards and visualize Business Central data in real time. With **Power Automate**, businesses can create workflows that automate repetitive tasks, such as sending approval notifications or updating records across systems. **Power Apps** allows organizations to build lightweight applications that extend Business Central's functionality, whether for internal processes or customer-facing apps. Together, these tools empower organizations to innovate quickly without heavy coding.

The integration extends further into **Azure services**. Business Central can connect with Azure Active Directory for secure identity management, ensuring users have the right permissions. It also leverages Azure's data storage, AI, and machine learning capabilities. For example, companies can use AI models to predict inventory needs, identify late payments, or generate insights into customer behavior. This makes Business Central more than just a transactional system; it becomes an intelligent platform that supports smarter decision-making.

This seamless integration is what makes Business Central stand out in the ERP market. Rather than being an isolated piece of software, it acts as the central hub of an organization's digital operations, plugged into the same ecosystem that powers collaboration, analytics, automation, and cloud innovation. For readers, understanding this bigger picture highlights why adopting Business Central is not just about choosing an ERP; it is about embracing a connected, modern workplace.

Tip   Don't overlook the small things, features like creating quotes directly in Outlook or exporting to Excel save huge amounts of time. Encourage users to explore these everyday integrations.

At the same time, Business Central maintains the flexibility to adapt to different industries and unique business processes. It comes with a rich set of standard features, but it can also be extended through Microsoft AppSource, where organizations can install add-ons built by partners.

Developers can create custom extensions using AL, the dedicated programming language for Business Central, allowing companies to tailor the system to their exact needs without disrupting the standard functionality.

Cloud vs. On-Premises

When organizations decide to adopt Business Central, one of the first choices they must make is how they want the system to be deployed. Microsoft offers Business Central in two primary models: cloud and on-premises. Both versions provide the same core functionality, but the way they are delivered, maintained, and paid for can make a big difference to the business. Understanding these differences is essential for making an informed decision.

In the **cloud model**, Business Central is hosted on Microsoft's servers and delivered over the internet as a subscription service. This means that companies do not need to worry about installing or maintaining the software on their own hardware. Updates, backups, and security are handled directly by Microsoft. New features are automatically rolled out on a regular basis, ensuring that the system stays up to date with the latest innovations. The cloud version also makes it easier for users to work from anywhere, whether in the office, at home, or on the move, because all they need is a browser or mobile app. For growing businesses, the cloud offers scalability; the system can expand as the organization adds more users, data, or locations without requiring large upfront investments in servers.

Important   Cloud and on-premises provide the *same core functionality*. The choice is about **how you want to manage costs, compliance, and IT resources**, not about losing features.

The **on-premises model**, by contrast, is installed and maintained on a company's own servers. This gives the organization full control over its data and its IT environment. Businesses that have strict regulatory requirements or operate in industries where data sovereignty is critical sometimes prefer this option. On-premises deployments also allow for deeper customization of the system, as the organization can choose exactly how the software is configured and integrated with other applications. However, this flexibility comes with added responsibility. The company's IT team must handle tasks such as installing updates, maintaining hardware, ensuring backups, and securing the environment against threats.

From a cost perspective, the cloud is usually offered as a subscription, with predictable monthly or annual fees. On-premises deployments often require a larger upfront investment in hardware and licenses, followed by ongoing maintenance costs. The decision often comes down to how the organization balances control, cost, and convenience. Smaller and fast-growing companies often find the cloud more attractive, while larger enterprises with established IT infrastructure sometimes lean toward on-premises deployments.

It is also worth noting that Microsoft continues to invest heavily in the cloud version of Business Central, ensuring it receives new features and AI-driven improvements first. On-premises users do receive updates, but these are less frequent and require more effort to implement. As a result, many organizations that start with on-premises eventually consider migrating to the cloud to take advantage of innovation and reduced maintenance overhead. The decision flow for choosing between cloud and on-premises deployment models is illustrated in Figure 1-2.

Tip   If you're unsure which to choose, start with the **Cloud version** in a pilot project. It's easier to set up and can help you test Business Central quickly before committing long-term.

In summary, both cloud and on-premises models offer the same strong core of Business Central, but they serve different needs. The cloud emphasizes flexibility, scalability, and convenience, while on-premises prioritizes control and customization. Choosing between them is not just a technical decision but also a strategic one, shaping how the business will operate and grow in the years to come.

Cloud vs. On-Premises: Key Differences

A side-by-side comparison of the two deployment models is shown in Table 1-1.

***Table 1-1.** Key differences between cloud and on-premises deployment*

Aspect	Cloud (Business Central Online)	On-Premises (Business Central Installed Locally)
Deployment	Hosted on Microsoft's servers, accessed via the internet	Installed on company's own servers and managed internally
Updates	Automatic, frequent updates from Microsoft	Manually by Microsoft partners with proper licenses; updates are less frequent and depend on partner scheduling
Cost Model	Subscription-based (monthly/annual fees)	Upfront license and hardware costs, object purchase costs for customizations, and yearly Business Ready Enhancement Plan (BREP) maintenance fees

(continued)

Table 1-1. (*continued*)

Aspect	Cloud (Business Central Online)	On-Premises (Business Central Installed Locally)
Scalability	Easy to scale, add users or storage instantly	Scaling requires additional hardware and IT effort
Maintenance	Managed by Microsoft (backups, patches, uptime)	Managed by the organization's IT staff
Accessibility	Available anywhere via browser or mobile app	Access limited to company network unless remote access is configured
Innovation	New features, AI tools, and integrations delivered first	Receives all core features but cannot use **cloud-only capabilities**
Customization	Flexible but within Microsoft's cloud framework	Allows deeper customizations and integrations, but non-cloud-optimized extensions (e.g., .NET, direct SQL, local file system) require additional yearly fees under the Universal Code Initiative (UCI)
Security	Enterprise-grade security handled by Microsoft	Security depends on internal IT team's capabilities
Data Control	Data stored in Microsoft's data centers	Data stored entirely within company infrastructure

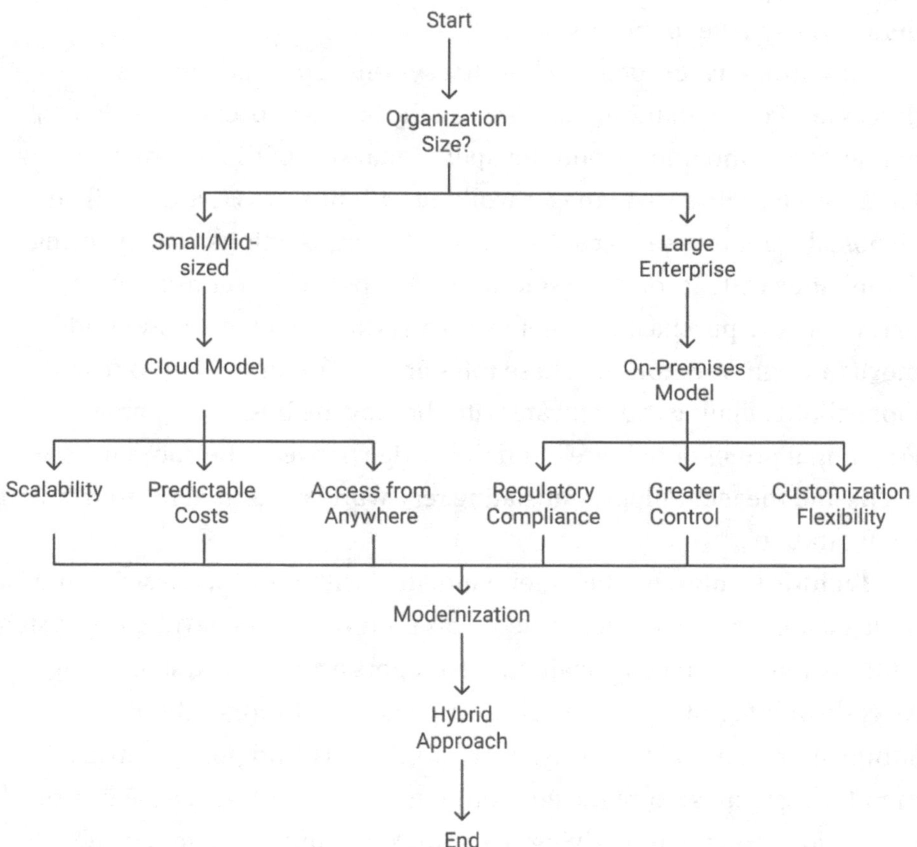

Figure 1-2. *Decision flow for choosing between cloud and on-premises deployment models in Business Central*

Functional vs. Technical Roles

Every successful Business Central implementation depends on people. While the software provides the tools, it is the individuals who configure, use, and maintain the system that bring it to life. To make sense of these responsibilities, it is useful to divide them into two broad categories:

functional roles and technical roles. Both are equally important, and together they ensure that Business Central is not just deployed but also delivers real value to the business.

Functional roles focus on how the system supports business processes. People in these roles are usually business users, consultants, or managers who understand the operational side of the organization. For example, a finance manager working with Business Central will be responsible for overseeing accounts, posting transactions, and ensuring compliance with accounting standards. A supply chain consultant may configure purchasing and inventory settings to reflect how goods move through warehouses. These roles are less about writing code and more about aligning the software with the way the business operates. Functional professionals are often the bridge between the company's needs and the technology, translating real-world requirements into system configurations.

Technical roles, on the other hand, deal with how Business Central is built, customized, and maintained. This group includes developers, system administrators, and IT specialists. Developers extend the system using AL code or integrate it with external applications through APIs. System administrators handle security, user permissions, and performance monitoring to make sure the environment runs smoothly. These technical experts focus on the underlying structure, ensuring the system is reliable, secure, and adaptable to future growth.

Although the distinction between functional and technical roles is clear, in practice, they work closely together. For instance, a functional consultant may identify the need for a custom report or a workflow automation that does not exist in the standard system. The consultant describes the requirement, and the developer translates it into a technical solution. Similarly, when new features are introduced, technical staff may rely on functional users to test them in real business scenarios. This collaboration ensures that the system not only works from a technical perspective but also truly supports business objectives.

Tip Functional users should learn the basics of navigation and setup, while technical users should spend time understanding real business processes. This overlap reduces miscommunication and speeds up projects.

It is also worth noting that the line between these roles is becoming more fluid. With the rise of low-code and no-code tools, functional users are increasingly able to design reports, dashboards, and simple automations without deep programming knowledge. At the same time, technical professionals are expected to understand business processes well enough to deliver meaningful solutions. This overlap creates a more agile environment where both groups share ownership of the system's success.

In summary, functional roles ensure that Business Central reflects business needs, while technical roles make sure it runs smoothly and can be extended when required. One without the other would leave gaps, but together they form the backbone of every Business Central project. For readers of this book, recognizing where they fit, whether functional, technical, or somewhere in between, will help them approach the platform with clarity and purpose. The main distinctions between functional and technical roles are highlighted in Table 1-2.

Table 1-2. *Functional vs. technical roles in Business Central*

Aspect	Functional Roles	Technical Roles
Focus Area	Business processes and daily operations	System configuration, customization, and maintenance
Typical Users	End users, consultants, managers	Developers, system administrators, IT staff
Key Responsibilities	Configuring modules (Finance, Sales, Purchasing, Inventory, etc.), setting up posting groups, defining workflows, testing business processes	Writing AL code, creating extensions, managing integrations (APIs, Power Platform), handling upgrades, maintaining security and performance
Skills Needed	Business process knowledge, analytical thinking, understanding of ERP workflows, reporting	Programming (AL, APIs), system architecture, database management, security, DevOps
Example Tasks	Setting up a Chart of Accounts, configuring approval workflows, creating user training, testing end-to-end transactions	Developing custom reports, integrating BC with a CRM, managing user permissions, automating backups
Goal	Ensure the system supports business needs and is easy to use	Ensure the system is stable, scalable, and adaptable
Interaction with Each Other	Defines requirements, validates solutions	Builds solutions, ensures technical feasibility

Business Central Licensing and User Access

Every user who signs in to Microsoft Dynamics 365 Business Central needs a license that defines what they can see and do. Understanding these license types helps businesses plan costs wisely and assign the right access for each employee. Table 1-3 shows the main licensing types in Business Central.

License Purchase Model

Business Central licenses are available only through Microsoft's **Cloud Solution Provider (CSP)** program.

Most organizations subscribe monthly or yearly rather than purchasing perpetual licenses. This keeps the software always current with Microsoft's regular updates.

Table 1-3. *Main license types*

License Type	Description	Typical Users	Key Capabilities
Essentials	Core ERP features, finance, sales, purchasing, inventory, and projects	Accountants, purchasing/sales staff	Daily operations and reporting for most SMBs.
Premium	Includes all Essentials features plus manufacturing and service management	Production planners, service managers	Advanced shop-floor and service contract management.
Team Member	Light-use license with read-only and limited update rights	Executives, managers, occasional users	View data, run reports, approve workflows, update timesheets, or expenses.
External Accountant	Free license for external auditors or accountants linked to the tenant	CPA/external accountant	Read and post in financial modules for review and audit.
Device	Shared license tied to one device rather than a user	Warehouse, POS, or shop-floor terminals	Multiple users can sign in on that device for scanning or job entry.

Trial and Evaluation Access

Microsoft lets prospects explore Business Central through a **30-day evaluation**, often called a *viral trial*. This trial can host up to **10,000 temporary users** for demonstrations or proof-of-concept projects. Once a paid license is assigned, the first licensed user who logs in automatically converts the environment into a production tenant.

Entitlements and Permissions

Business Central Online no longer uses classic license files (.flf). Instead, access is governed by **Entitlements** – rules stored in Microsoft Entra ID that map to each service plan (Essentials, Premium, etc.).

If a user holds a *Team Member* license, even assigning the **SUPER** permission set won't grant access beyond their entitlement scope.

Microsoft 365 Read-Only Access

Users with certain Microsoft 365 licenses can view shared Business Central data directly inside Teams or Outlook for collaboration, without needing a full BC license.

How Licensing Works Behind the Scenes

Business Central Online no longer uses the old Dynamics NAV ".flf" license files.

Instead, Microsoft applies an *entitlement model* managed through **Microsoft Entra ID (Azure AD)**.

Each license (Essentials, Premium, etc.) maps to a specific **service plan**, and that plan determines the *entitlements* – the exact tables, pages, and features a user can access.

Even if an administrator mistakenly gives a *Team Member* the **SUPER** permission set, the user still can't open pages or post entries restricted by their entitlement.

Entitlements always override permission sets.

Example Scenario: Choosing the Right Mix

Contoso Fabrics Ltd. is a growing textile manufacturer with 45 employees.

Department	Users	License Choice	Reason
Finance	4	**Essentials**	Need accounting, purchasing, and banking features only.
Production	6	**Premium**	Must access the Manufacturing module for shop-floor control.
Sales and Service	10	**Essentials**	Manage sales orders, quotes, and inventory.
Management and Executives	5	**Team Member**	Review KPIs, approve purchases, run reports.
External Auditor	1	**External Accountant**	Periodic review without extra cost.
Warehouse Devices	3 shared stations	**Device Licenses (3)**	Three tablets used for barcode scanning and item picking.

Outcome

By mixing license types, Contoso pays only for what each role truly needs while ensuring everyone can do their job efficiently.

Finance and Sales enjoy full functionality; managers can review performance; shop-floor staff record production; the auditor logs in securely when required.

Practical Use Case

Use Case: Approving a Purchase Invoice

- A purchasing agent with an **Essentials** license creates a Purchase Invoice and posts it.

- A manager with a **Team Member** license receives an approval notification in Teams, opens the document, reviews it, and approves it.

- An external accountant logs in later using their free license to verify postings and export the Trial Balance for auditing.

Each role interacts with the same transaction but at an access level appropriate to their license.

Microsoft 365 Read-Only Access

Some employees who don't have Business Central licenses can still view shared data inside **Microsoft Teams** or **Outlook** through their existing Microsoft 365 subscription.

This feature allows organization-wide collaboration without extra ERP licenses – ideal for departments like HR or Marketing that occasionally need to see business records.

Best Practices

- **Match roles to needs.** Not everyone requires a full license.

- **Review entitlements after updates.** New features may shift license boundaries.

- **Plan for seasonal workers.** Device or Team Member licenses keep costs predictable.

- **Keep administrators full users.** The first login after license purchase should be a licensed full user to convert any trial into production.

Tip   Licensing defines *what* areas of Business Central a user can access.

Permission sets define *what actions* they can perform within those areas.

Combine both thoughtfully for secure and efficient user management.

Navigation Tips

One of the strengths of Business Central is its user-friendly design. However, for someone new to the platform, the number of menus, actions, and role-based pages can feel overwhelming at first. Learning how to navigate efficiently not only saves time but also makes the experience smoother and more enjoyable.

Business Central is built around the concept of **Role Centers**. A Role Center acts as the landing page, showing the most relevant information for a user's role. For example, an accountant will see financial data, tasks, and links specific to accounting, while a sales manager will see opportunities, customers, and sales orders. From here, users can access the rest of the system.

The **navigation bar and action ribbon** are key tools. The navigation bar, found at the top, allows quick movement between modules like Finance, Sales, and Purchasing. The action ribbon (sometimes called the command bar) changes depending on the page you are on and provides shortcuts to common actions such as posting, printing, or creating new records.

Another powerful tool is the **Tell Me** search box (shortcut: Alt+Q). Instead of remembering exactly where a page is located, users can type keywords like "Customer Ledger" or "Chart of Accounts" and instantly jump to the page, report, or action they need. This search also offers links to documentation, making it easier to learn as you go.

Users can also **personalize their workspace**. This includes rearranging tiles on the Role Center, hiding fields they don't use, or adding new shortcuts for frequent tasks. Personalization helps reduce clutter and ensures that users focus only on the tools that matter most to them.

For those who want to be even more efficient, Business Central offers **keyboard shortcuts and quick actions**. Knowing these can significantly reduce reliance on the mouse and make repetitive tasks faster. Some of the most useful shortcuts are listed in Table 1-4.

Table 1-4. *Handy keyboard shortcuts in Business Central*

Action	Shortcut
Open **Tell Me** (search)	Alt+Q
Open **New Document** (on list pages)	Alt+N
Refresh page	F5
Open or close **FastTab**	Alt+Shift+Arrow Down/Up
Switch between lines in a list	Arrow Up/Down
Drill down into a field	Alt+Down Arrow
Expand or collapse FactBox pane	Alt+F2
Copy value in a field	Ctrl+C
Paste value in a field	Ctrl+V
Select multiple records	Ctrl+Click or Shift+Click
Zoom into a field (show full text)	Shift+F2
Close current page	Esc
Search/filter list	Ctrl+F
Clear filter	Ctrl+Shift+F
Open My Settings	Alt+T (from Role Center)

Additional Navigation Tips

- **Use Bookmarks:** You can bookmark any page and pin it to your Role Center for one-click access.

- **FactBoxes Are Your Friend:** On many pages, FactBoxes show related details (like customer balance or vendor history) without needing to leave the page.

- **Filters and Saved Views:** When working with lists (e.g., customers, vendors), apply filters and save them as views so you can reuse them later.

- **Notifications:** Pay attention to notifications at the top of the page; these often guide you to complete tasks or fix errors.

- **Mobile and Tablet Apps:** Navigation on mobile devices is simplified, but the same Role Center structure applies, so practice on the web helps you on the go.

Tip   Start by bookmarking two to three pages you use the most (like Sales Invoices, Chart of Accounts, or Purchase Orders) to save clicks.

Key Module Snapshots

Business Central is made up of several modules, each designed to manage a specific area of the business. While every company may use different combinations depending on their needs, it is useful to understand the most important modules at a high level. Think of this as a guided walk-through of the core building blocks of the system. An overview of the core Business Central modules is presented in Figure 1-3.

Business Central Modules Overview

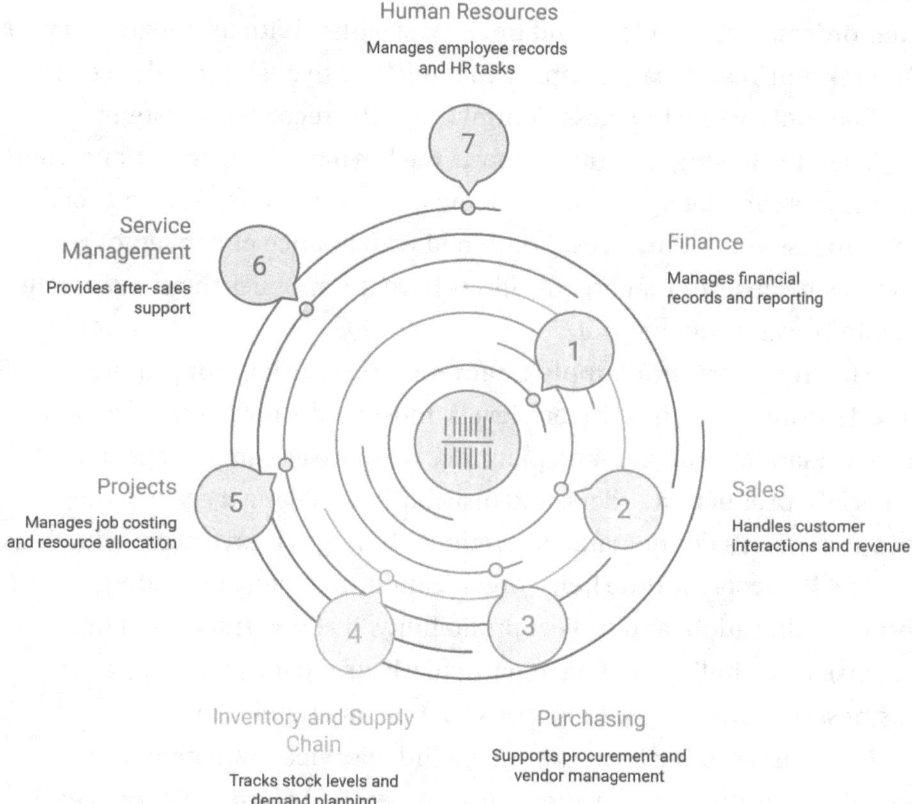

Figure 1-3. *Business Central modules overview, showing core areas such as Finance, Sales, Purchasing, Inventory, Projects, Service Management, and Human Resources*

The **Finance module** is at the heart of Business Central. This is where companies manage their general ledger, accounts receivable, accounts payable, bank accounts, and fixed assets. The finance area provides tools for budgeting, cash flow forecasting, and generating reports such as trial balances, profit and loss statements, and balance sheets. For many organizations, this is the starting point, as it ensures accurate financial records and compliance with reporting standards.

The **Sales module** handles everything related to customers and revenue. Users can manage customer records, create quotes, process sales orders, issue invoices, and track receivables. With its integration into Outlook and Teams, salespeople can interact with customers directly from familiar tools, while Business Central keeps the records consistent.

The **Purchasing module** supports the buying side of operations. Here, businesses can manage vendors, create purchase orders, receive goods, and process vendor invoices. Combined with finance and inventory, purchasing ensures that organizations have the supplies they need while keeping costs under control.

The **Inventory and Supply Chain module** is crucial for product-based businesses. It tracks stock levels, movements between warehouses, item availability, and demand planning. Businesses can manage bills of materials, production orders, and distribution, making it easier to align inventory with sales demand and reduce shortages or overstock situations.

The **Projects module** helps organizations manage job costing, resource allocation, and project profitability. It allows tracking of time, expenses, and billing, making it particularly useful for service-oriented businesses such as consulting, construction, or engineering.

Other areas of Business Central include **Service Management** for organizations that provide after-sales support and **Human Resources** for managing employee records and basic HR tasks. While these may not be core for every organization, they provide additional value for those that require them.

Taken together, these modules provide a complete picture of a company's operations. Data flows seamlessly between them: a sales order impacts inventory, which in turn triggers purchasing and updates financial records. This connected approach eliminates silos and gives decision-makers a clear, real-time view of the entire business.

Conclusion

This opening chapter has laid the groundwork for understanding Microsoft Dynamics 365 Business Central. We began with an overview of the platform, exploring its history, evolution, and how it connects seamlessly with the broader Microsoft ecosystem. We then looked at the two deployment options, cloud and on-premises, understanding their strengths and trade-offs. The distinction between functional and technical roles was clarified, showing how both groups collaborate to make implementations successful. Readers were also guided through navigation tips, learning about Role Centers, shortcuts, and personalization. Finally, we took a high-level tour of the core modules, gaining a snapshot of how Finance, Sales, Purchasing, Inventory, and Projects fit together.

By the end of this chapter, readers should feel oriented within the world of Business Central. They now know where the system came from, what it looks like, who uses it, and how to move around confidently. This foundation prepares them to dive deeper into the modules, processes, and customization options explored in the following chapters.

Chapter Highlights

- Business Central is Microsoft's modern ERP solution, evolved from Navision and Dynamics NAV.

- It integrates seamlessly with Microsoft 365, Power Platform, and Azure, making it part of a larger digital ecosystem.

- Two deployment models are available: **cloud** (scalable, low maintenance) and **on-premises** (greater control, higher IT responsibility).

- Roles are divided into **functional** (business process users and consultants) and **technical** (developers and administrators).

- Navigation is user-friendly, with **Role Centers**, **Tell Me search (Alt+Q)**, personalization, and keyboard shortcuts boosting productivity.

- Key modules include **Finance, Sales, Purchasing, Inventory, and Projects**, with Service Management and HR as optional extensions.

- Basic terms such as **Company, Environment, Posting, Ledger Entries, and Dimensions** form the foundation for understanding data flow in Business Central.

Self-Check Questions

1. What is Microsoft Dynamics 365 Business Central, and how did it evolve from Navision and Dynamics NAV?

2. Name two advantages of using Business Central in the cloud and two reasons why some businesses may still prefer on-premises.

3. How do functional roles and technical roles differ, and why do they need to work closely together?

4. What is the purpose of the **Tell Me (Alt+Q)** search feature in Business Central?

5. Define the terms **Posting, Ledger Entries, and Dimensions** with a simple example of each.

Self-Check Answers

1. **What is Microsoft Dynamics 365 Business Central, and how did it evolve from Navision and Dynamics NAV?**

    Business Central is Microsoft's modern ERP solution for small and mid-sized businesses. It started as **Navision** in the 1980s (developed in Denmark), became **Microsoft Dynamics NAV** after Microsoft's acquisition in 2002, and evolved into **Dynamics 365 Business Central** in 2018 as a cloud-first solution.

2. **Name two advantages of using Business Central in the cloud and two reasons why some businesses may still prefer on-premises.**

    - **Cloud Advantages:** Automatic updates, scalability, predictable subscription costs, and access from anywhere

    - **On-Premises Reasons:** Strict compliance or regulatory needs, deeper customization, and full control over data and infrastructure

3. **How do functional roles and technical roles differ, and why do they need to work closely together?**

    - **Functional roles** focus on business processes (e.g., accountants, consultants) – they configure workflows and ensure the system fits business needs.

    - **Technical roles** focus on system setup and customization (e.g., developers, admins) – they build extensions, manage integrations, and maintain security.

- They need to collaborate because functional users define *what the business needs*, while technical users make it *technically possible.*

4. **What is the purpose of the Tell Me (Alt+Q) search feature in Business Central?**

   The **Tell Me** feature helps users quickly find pages, reports, or actions by typing keywords instead of navigating menus. For example, typing "Chart of Accounts" in Tell Me instantly opens that page. It saves time and reduces confusion for new users.

5. **Define the terms Posting, Ledger Entries, and Dimensions with a simple example of each.**

   - **Posting:** Finalizing a transaction so it is recorded in the system. *Example: Posting a sales invoice updates customer balances, inventory, and the general ledger.*

   - **Ledger Entries:** Permanent records created after posting. *Example: Posting a vendor invoice creates a Vendor Ledger Entry and a General Ledger Entry.*

   - **Dimensions:** Tags added to transactions for deeper reporting. *Example: Assigning a Department dimension = "Sales" when posting travel expenses, so reports show which department spent it.*

Practical Exercises

Follow these steps in your Business Central **Sandbox Environment** to practice the concepts from this chapter:

1. **Log In to a Sandbox Environment**

   - If you don't already have one, ask your administrator to create a sandbox environment.

   - Open a sample company like *Cronus USA, Inc.* (provided by Microsoft for training).

2. **Explore Navigation**

   - On the Role Center page, look at the tiles and cues designed for your role.

   - Use the **Tell Me (Alt + Q)** search bar to look for the *Chart of Accounts* and open it.

3. **Create and Post a Transaction**

   - Go to the **Sales Invoices** page.

   - Create a new invoice for a sample customer (e.g., *Adatum Corporation*).

   - Add a line for any item in the system.

   - Review the totals and click **Post**.

4. **Review Ledger Entries**

   - After posting, use **Tell Me** to search for *Customer Ledger Entries*.

   - Open the entries and verify that your invoice created a record.

   - Optionally, check the **General Ledger Entries** to see the financial impact.

5. **Apply Dimensions**

- Go back to your posted invoice and check if you can assign a **Dimension** (e.g., Department = *Sales*).

- Later, try filtering Customer Ledger Entries by Dimension to see the analysis capability.

CHAPTER 2

Functional Essentials

This chapter introduces the functional backbone of Business Central that every consultant and user must understand before moving to advanced scenarios. It focuses on the finance, sales, and purchase processes that shape day-to-day business operations. By exploring the key elements, such as the chart of accounts, posting groups, journals, dimensions, and approvals, you will gain a clear picture of how Business Central handles financial integrity and operational flows.

We begin with the **chart of accounts and posting groups**, which define how transactions are classified and mapped to the correct accounts. This section shows how structure and rules ensure accurate reporting and compliance. Next, we move into the **sales and purchase cycles**, where you will learn how quotes, orders, invoices, and payments are connected, forming an end-to-end workflow for managing customers and vendors.

The chapter then shifts to **journals and dimensions**, essential tools for recording transactions and enriching data with analytical tags. Understanding these concepts helps you move beyond basic bookkeeping and into meaningful analysis that supports management decisions. Finally, we close with **document approvals**, highlighting how Business Central ensures control, accountability, and compliance through workflow-driven authorization.

By the end of this chapter, you will have a strong foundation in the functional essentials of Business Central. These fundamentals are not only required for smooth daily operations but also serve as the stepping stones for advanced features and integrations that you will explore later in this book.

© Dr. Gomathi S 2025

Dr. Gomathi S, *Microsoft Dynamics 365 Business Central Essentials*, Apress Pocket Guides, https://doi.org/10.1007/979-8-8688-2229-2_2

Basic Terminology in Business Central

To make the most of Business Central, it is important to understand a few common terms that you will encounter frequently. These concepts may sound simple, but they form the backbone of how the system works.

Important   If you're just exploring Business Central, ask your administrator to create a sandbox environment for you. That way, you can practice freely without touching real business data.

A **company** in Business Central represents a complete set of business data. For example, an organization might have a live company called *Contoso Ltd.* and another test company called *Contoso Test*. Each company has its own chart of accounts, customers, vendors, and transactions. Companies are useful when managing multiple subsidiaries, different legal entities, or even separate test data sets.

First-time user note   Remember that environments are separate. If you create data in your sandbox environment, it won't show up in production, and that's a good thing when you're learning.

A tenant is the higher-level container that can include one or more environments. Each environment represents a separate Business Central instance that can contain multiple companies within it. For instance, you might have a *Production Environment* where live business data is maintained and a *Sandbox Environment* used only for testing or training purposes. The benefit of environments is that they allow businesses to experiment or train staff without affecting live operations.

Important   Think of ledger entries as a permanent diary. Even if you correct something later, the original entry will still be there for tracking.

The term **posting** refers to finalizing a transaction so that it becomes part of the system's permanent records. For example, when a sales order is posted, Business Central updates the customer's outstanding balance, records the revenue in the general ledger, and adjusts inventory levels. Posting ensures that transactions are locked in place and reflected in financial reports, making them accurate and reliable.

When a transaction is posted, it generates **ledger entries**, which are the detailed records of what happened. For instance, posting a vendor invoice creates entries in both the Vendor Ledger and the General Ledger. These entries provide traceability and serve as an audit trail, since they cannot be deleted, only corrected or adjusted. This gives businesses confidence that their financial history is secure and transparent.

Important   Once you post, you cannot "un-post." If you make a mistake, you'll need to reverse or correct it with a new entry. Always double-check before clicking *Post*.

Finally, **dimensions** are tags that can be attached to transactions for more detailed reporting and analysis. Instead of creating thousands of accounts, dimensions allow businesses to classify transactions by categories such as *Department* (Sales, Finance, Operations) or *Region* (North, South). For example, a travel expense can be posted to the general ledger with a *Department Dimension* set to "Marketing." Later, managers can analyze costs by department without needing to change the chart of accounts.

Important   If your reports look too generic, dimensions are probably the missing piece. Make sure to apply them consistently to get powerful insights later.

Together, these terms, company, environment, posting, ledger entries, and dimensions, form the foundation of how data flows in Business Central. These common terms and their examples are summarized in Table 2-1. Companies and environments define where the data lives, posting and ledger entries ensure accuracy and permanence, and dimensions provide the flexibility to analyze information in ways that make sense for decision-makers.

Table 2-1. *Basic terminology in Business Central*

Terminology	Definition	Example
Chart of Accounts (COA)	A list of all accounts used to record financial transactions.	Accounts like *1000 – Cash*, *2000 – Accounts Payable*, *4000 – Sales Revenue*.
Journal	A worksheet where you enter transactions before posting.	Entering payroll expenses into the *General Journal* before posting.
Posting Groups	Rules that tell the system which accounts to use when posting transactions.	Customer Posting Group "DOMESTIC" directs sales invoices to domestic revenue accounts.
Master Data	Core records that do not change often but are used across the system.	Customer cards, vendor cards, and item cards.

(continued)

Table 2-1. (*continued*)

Terminology	Definition	Example
Document	A transaction form in the system that can be posted.	A *Sales Order* document that becomes a posted shipment and posted invoice after posting.
Batch	A group of transactions entered together in a journal.	A batch called *January Expenses* in the General Journal.
Trial Balance	A report showing the total debits and credits of all accounts.	A year-end trial balance used to verify financial accuracy.
Dimensions Value	The specific option chosen within a dimension.	For Dimension "Department," values might be *Finance*, *Sales*, *Operations*.
FactBox	A pane on the side of a page showing related information.	On the Customer Card, the FactBox shows *Outstanding Balance*.
Role Center	A personalized homepage tailored to a user's role.	An *Accountant Role Center* showing cash balances and journals.

Chart of Accounts and Posting Groups

At the heart of any financial system lies the chart of accounts, and Business Central is no exception. The chart of accounts acts as the backbone for recording and reporting all financial activity. Each account represents a category, such as assets, liabilities, income, or expenses, and together they create a structured framework for tracking the health of the business. A well-designed chart of accounts makes it easy for users to enter transactions correctly and for decision-makers to review accurate financial statements.

Posting groups work hand in hand with the chart of accounts. Instead of asking users to decide the correct account every time, posting groups apply predefined rules that automatically direct entries to the right place. For example, when you raise a sales invoice, the system uses the customer's posting group to know which revenue account should be updated. Similarly, vendor posting groups control how purchases are posted to expense or liability accounts.

Important   The chart of accounts is the backbone of financial reporting; set it up carefully before starting transactions.

By combining a structured chart of accounts with smart posting group rules, Business Central ensures consistency, accuracy, and efficiency. This setup reduces manual errors, speeds up transaction entry, and guarantees that all reports draw from reliable financial data.

The chart of accounts (COA) and posting groups form the foundation of financial management in Business Central. Without these two elements, it would be impossible to record, classify, and report business transactions in a reliable way. While the chart of accounts provides the structure for storing financial data, posting groups act as the rules that tell the system where each transaction should land. Together, they simplify the process of financial recording and ensure accuracy across the system.

Chart of Accounts

The **chart of accounts (COA)** is a complete list of the general ledger (G/L) accounts that define how transactions are categorized. These accounts are arranged in a logical order, assets first, followed by liabilities, equity, income, and expenses. Each account has a unique number and name, making it easy to identify and use. This end-to-end posting process is illustrated in Figure 2-1.

- **Purpose:** To organize financial data so businesses can generate balance sheets, income statements, and other financial reports.

- **Structure:** Typically starts with higher-level categories (e.g., 10000–19999 for assets) and drills down into detailed accounts (e.g., 10100 for bank accounts).

- **Flexibility:** Business Central allows you to customize the numbering system and add new accounts as needed.

Example

A company may use

- **10100 – Main Bank Account**

- **20100 – Trade Payables**

- **40100 – Sales Revenue (Domestic)**

- **50100 – Office Supplies Expense**

This arrangement makes it easy to see at a glance where money is coming from and where it is going.

Posting Groups

While the chart of accounts provides structure, **posting groups** reduce manual effort by automatically mapping transactions to the correct G/L accounts. Instead of users choosing accounts each time, posting groups use predefined logic to guide transactions.

There are different types of posting groups:

- **General Posting Groups:** Define how customers, vendors, items, and resources interact with accounts. For example, a domestic customer may be mapped to a local sales revenue account, while an export customer may be linked to an overseas revenue account.

- **Customer Posting Groups:** Decide which receivable accounts customer transactions are posted to.

- **Vendor Posting Groups:** Decide which payable accounts vendor transactions are posted to.

- **Inventory Posting Groups:** Map items to their respective inventory, cost, and adjustment accounts.

- **Bank Posting Groups:** Define how bank transactions are recorded.

Tip   Assign **default posting groups** to customers, vendors, and items to reduce manual errors.

By combining these, Business Central can handle complex posting needs without burdening the user with constant account selections. *Examples of posting groups and their mappings are shown in Table 2-2.*

Table 2-2. *Examples of posting groups and their mapped G/L accounts in Business Central*

Type of Posting Group	Example Name	Mapped G/L Account	Purpose
Customer Posting Group	DOMESTIC	20100 – Trade Receivables (Domestic)	Directs customer invoices to the receivables account.
Vendor Posting Group	LOCAL	30100 – Trade Payables (Local)	Posts vendor invoices to the correct payable account.

(continued)

Table 2-2. (*continued*)

Type of Posting Group	Example Name	Mapped G/L Account	Purpose
General Business Posting Group	EXPORT	40200 – Export Sales Revenue	Links customer business type to revenue accounts.
General Product Posting Group	ELECTRONICS	50200 – Electronics COGS	Ensures items sold post to proper revenue and cost accounts.
Inventory Posting Group	FINISHED GOODS	15100 – Finished Goods Inventory	Reduces inventory and posts to COGS when sales occur.
Bank Posting Group	MAIN BANK	10100 – Main Bank Account	Ensures receipts and payments are posted to the right bank.

This shows how different posting groups together ensure that each transaction finds its way to the right G/L account.

Figure 2-1. *Sales invoice posting process: how Business Central uses posting groups (Customer, Business, Product, Inventory) to automatically update receivables, revenue, VAT, inventory, and COGS accounts when an invoice is posted*

How They Work Together

Think of the **chart of accounts** as the destination and **posting groups** as the GPS. The chart of accounts lists all possible destinations (accounts), while posting groups automatically choose the right path for each type of transaction. Some best practices are summarized in Figure 2-2.

Real-Life Workflow Example

Scenario: Posting a Sales Invoice

1. A user creates a sales invoice for a domestic customer who bought ten units of an item.

2. The **Customer Posting Group** attached to that customer is "DOMESTIC," which points to the "Trade Receivables (Domestic)" account.

3. The **General Business Posting Group** (customer side) and the **General Product Posting Group** (item side) work together. Their combination tells Business Central which revenue account and VAT account to update.

4. The **Inventory Posting Group** linked to the item ensures that the inventory value decreases from the correct stock account.

5. When the invoice is posted:

   - Debit ➤ Trade Receivables (Customer Posting Group)

   - Credit ➤ Sales Revenue (General Posting Group)

   - Credit ➤ VAT Payable (General Posting Group, if applicable)

- Credit ➤ Inventory (Inventory Posting Group)

- Debit ➤ Cost of Goods Sold (Inventory Posting Group)

This entire posting process happens automatically in the background, guided by posting groups, ensuring no user error in choosing accounts.

Benefits of Using COA and Posting Groups

- **Consistency:** Every transaction follows the same rules.

- **Efficiency:** Users save time as they don't have to manually select accounts.

- **Accuracy:** Financial reports remain reliable and error-free.

- **Flexibility:** Businesses can set up posting groups for different geographies, product lines, or industries.

- **Compliance:** Ensures proper mapping of taxes, revenue, and costs for audit readiness.

Common Challenges

- **Too Many Accounts:** Some companies overcomplicate their COA, making it hard to manage.

- **Incorrect Mapping:** Posting groups not properly set up can cause transactions to hit the wrong accounts.

- **Lack of Training:** Users unaware of how posting groups work may find it confusing when reports don't match expectations.

Best Practices

How to effectively manage COA and posting groups?

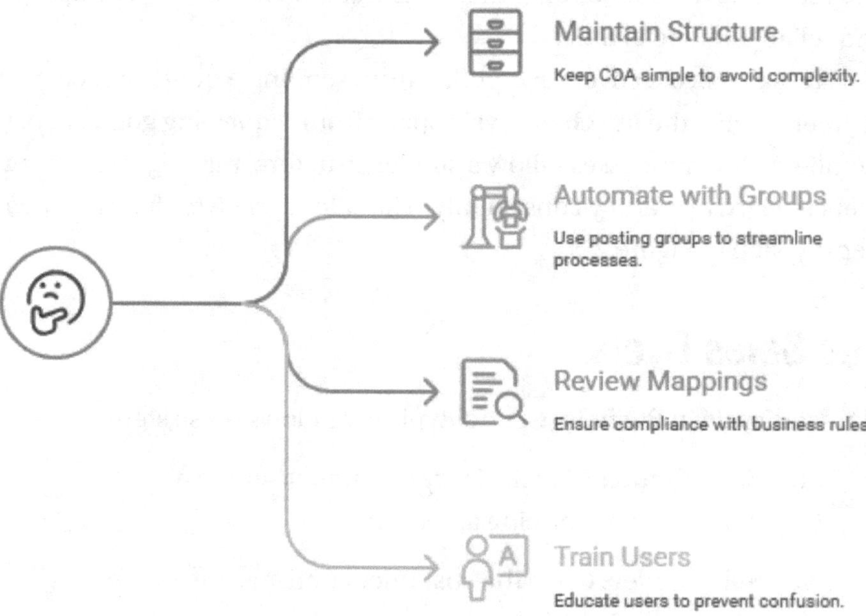

Figure 2-2. *Best practices for managing the chart of accounts (COA) and posting groups: maintain structure, automate with groups, review mappings regularly, and train users to ensure accuracy and compliance*

- Keep the chart of accounts structured and not overly detailed.

- Use posting groups to automate as much as possible.

- Regularly review account mappings to ensure compliance with business rules.

- Train users on how COA and posting groups interact to avoid confusion.

Sales/Purchase Cycle

Every business relies on two critical flows: **sales** (bringing in revenue from customers) and **purchases** (acquiring goods or services from vendors). In Business Central, these cycles are tightly connected to finance, inventory, and reporting. Understanding them ensures smooth day-to-day operations and reliable financial data.

The **sales cycle** covers everything from sending a quote to receiving payment, while the **purchase cycle** spans from requesting goods to paying suppliers. Both processes follow a similar structure, making it easier for users to learn and apply consistently. The sales cycle workflow is shown step-by-step in Figure 2-3.

The Sales Cycle

The sales cycle in Business Central typically follows these steps:

1. **Sales Quote:** A preliminary document sent to a customer with pricing and terms.

2. **Sales Order:** Once the customer confirms, the quote is converted into an order.

3. **Shipment:** Goods are shipped or services are delivered.

4. **Sales Invoice:** The order is invoiced; revenue and taxes are posted.

5. **Customer Payment:** Payment is received and applied to the customer's account.

Example

- A customer requests 50 laptops.

- You send a **sales quote** with price and delivery details.

- The customer accepts ➤ you create a **sales order**.

- Once delivered, you record a **shipment**.

- A **sales invoice** is generated, updating revenue and receivables.

- Finally, the customer pays, and the **bank account** and **receivables** are updated automatically.

Posting groups (explained in the earlier section) make sure each step hits the correct G/L accounts.

The Purchase Cycle

The purchase cycle mirrors the sales cycle, but from the vendor's perspective:

1. **Purchase Quote:** Request a price and terms from a vendor.

2. **Purchase Order:** Confirm the purchase and terms.

3. **Receipt:** Goods are received or services are acknowledged.

4. **Purchase Invoice:** Vendor invoice is entered and matched with the order/receipt.

5. **Vendor Payment:** Payment is made to the vendor.

Example

- Your company needs 100 office chairs.

- You request a **purchase quote** from a vendor.

- After approval, a **purchase order** is created.

- When chairs arrive, you post a **receipt** to update inventory.

- You receive a **purchase invoice** from the vendor, which updates expenses and liabilities.

- Finally, you pay the vendor, and the system reduces your **bank account balance** and **vendor payables**.

How Sales and Purchases Connect

Both cycles link directly to **finance** and **inventory**:

- Sales reduce inventory and increase revenue.

- Purchases increase inventory and create expenses or assets.

- Payments (from customers or to vendors) update bank balances and settle open entries.

Important   Both cycles follow the same five-step process: *Quote* ➤ *Order* ➤ *Delivery/Receipt* ➤ *Invoice* ➤ *Payment.*

Together, they form the lifeblood of Business Central's financial and operational system.

Visual Workflow

Sales Cycle Flow

Order Fulfillment Process

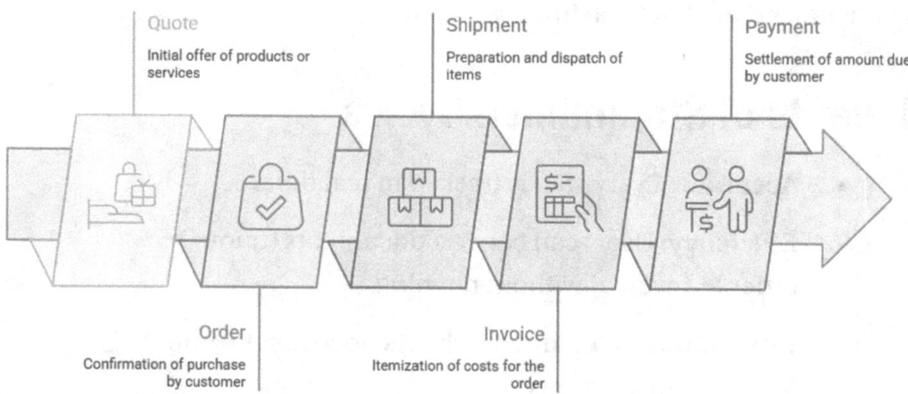

Figure 2-3. *Order fulfillment process: the step-by-step sales cycle in Business Central, starting from Quote and Order, followed by Shipment and Invoice, and ending with Payment from the customer*

Purchase Cycle Flow

Quote ➤ Order ➤ Receipt ➤ Invoice ➤ Payment

Tip   You can visualize both cycles side-by-side to show the mirror-like process.

Real-Life Use Case

Imagine a retail company selling electronics:

- **Sales Side:** A customer orders a smartphone ➤ Sales order created ➤ Phone shipped ➤ Sales invoice posted ➤ Customer pays.

- **Purchase Side:** To replenish stock, the company orders more smartphones from the supplier ➤ Purchase order created ➤ Stock received ➤ Vendor invoice posted ➤ Vendor paid.

This closed loop ensures the company always knows what is sold, what is bought, and the financial impact on profit.

Benefits of Streamlined Cycles

- **Accuracy:** Every step is tracked in real time.

- **Efficiency:** Users can convert documents (quote ➤ order ➤ invoice) without retyping.

- **Integration:** Sales and purchases flow directly into finance and inventory.

- **Visibility:** Management gets up-to-date views of cash flow, receivables, and payables.

Sales vs. Purchase Cycle Comparison

A side-by-side comparison of the two cycles is given in Table 2-3.

Table 2-3. *Comparison of sales and purchase cycles in Business Central*

Stage	Sales Cycle (Customer-Facing)	Purchase Cycle (Vendor-Facing)
1. Quote	Sales quote ➤ Offer sent to customer	Purchase quote ➤ Request sent to vendor
2. Order	Sales order ➤ Customer confirms purchase	Purchase order ➤ Company confirms purchase
3. Delivery/ Receipt	Shipment ➤ Goods/services delivered to customer	Receipt ➤ Goods/services received from vendor
4. Invoice	Sales invoice ➤ Revenue recorded, receivable created	Purchase invoice ➤ Expense/asset recorded, payable created
5. Payment	Customer payment ➤ Cash received, receivable cleared	Vendor payment ➤ Cash paid, payable cleared

Common Challenges

- Not applying customer/vendor payments properly leaves open entries.

- Poor setup of posting groups may send entries to the wrong accounts.

Best Practices

- Train users to follow the complete cycle, not skip steps.

- Use approval workflows for large sales or purchase orders.

- Regularly reconcile customer/vendor balances with the G/L.

- Automate recurring sales and purchase orders where possible.

The sales and purchase cycles are the heartbeat of Business Central. They connect customers, vendors, inventory, and finance into one seamless process. By mastering these workflows, businesses ensure accuracy in their operations and reliability in their financial reporting.

Case Study: ElectroMax Traders

Background

ElectroMax Traders is a mid-sized company that sells consumer electronics. They buy stock from international vendors and sell to retail customers. Let's see how both the sales and purchase cycles play out for a single product, the latest laptop model.

Sales Cycle in Action

1. **Sales Quote:** A retail customer asks for a price on 20 laptops. The sales team sends a quote with details.

2. **Sales Order:** The customer accepts, and the sales quote is converted to an order.

3. **Shipment:** Laptops are picked from inventory and shipped.

4. **Sales Invoice:** An invoice is posted, updating the G/L:

   - Debit ➤ Trade Receivables (customer)
   - Credit ➤ Sales Revenue
   - Credit ➤ VAT Payable (if applicable)
   - Debit ➤ Cost of Goods Sold (COGS)
   - Credit ➤ Inventory

5. **Customer Payment:** The customer pays within 15 days. The system clears receivables and updates the bank account.

Purchase Cycle in Action

1. **Purchase Quote:** To refill stock, ElectroMax requests pricing from its vendor.

2. **Purchase Order:** The vendor confirms the order for 100 laptops.

3. **Receipt:** The laptops arrive, and a warehouse receipt is posted, increasing inventory.

4. **Purchase Invoice:** The vendor invoice is received and posted:

   - Debit ➤ Inventory (or Expense)

   - Debit ➤ Input VAT (if applicable)

   - Credit ➤ Trade Payables (vendor)

5. **Vendor Payment:** ElectroMax pays the vendor after 30 days, reducing payables and bank balance.

How Both Cycles Connect

- When ElectroMax sells laptops, stock decreases, and revenue is recorded.

- When it purchases new laptops, stock increases, and liabilities are recorded.

- Together, these flows ensure the company always has visibility on **inventory levels, receivables, payables, cash flow, and profitability.**

Learning Point: Sales and purchase cycles are like two sides of the same coin. One brings revenue, the other ensures supply. Business Central links them seamlessly, giving management a full picture of business performance.

Journals and Dimensions

In Business Central, day-to-day financial and operational entries are captured through **journals**, while **dimensions** enrich those entries with additional meaning for reporting and analysis. Journals are like digital registers where transactions are entered, reviewed, and posted.

Dimensions, on the other hand, act like tags or labels that let you slice and analyze data beyond standard accounting reports. Together, they give organizations flexibility to record, classify, and analyze transactions in a controlled and meaningful way.

Important   Dimensions enrich transactions without complicating the chart of accounts.

Journals in Business Central

A journal is a worksheet for entering financial transactions before posting them to the general ledger. They are commonly used for recurring tasks such as payments, accruals, adjustments, and corrections. However, journals serve a much broader purpose; they form the backbone of the entire financial system. Any entry to any ledger in Business Central can only occur through a journal.

For smaller businesses that do not use the full sales and purchase document processes, journals can also be used to record sales and purchase transactions directly, achieving the same accounting impact. Even when sales or purchase documents are posted, the system first records the transactions in journals before posting them to their respective ledgers. Instead of directly editing the G/L, journals provide a controlled environment where users can review, validate, and ensure the accuracy of entries before final posting.

Common Types of Journals

- **General Journal:** For ad hoc entries such as corrections, adjustments, or allocations

- **Cash Receipt Journal:** To record money received from customers or other sources

- **Payment Journal:** To record outgoing payments to vendors or expenses

- **Item Journal:** For inventory adjustments, transfers, or opening balances

- **Fixed Asset Journal:** For depreciation, acquisitions, or disposals

Example

- A company needs to record monthly electricity expenses.

- The accountant opens a **General Journal**, enters the vendor's name, expense account, and amount, then posts.

- The entry updates the G/L with expense and liability accounts, keeping financial statements accurate.

Dimensions

While journals capture the "what" of a transaction, **dimensions** capture the "context." A dimension is a code that adds another layer of detail to financial entries, such as which department, project, region, or product line the cost belongs to.

Why Dimensions Matter

- They allow businesses to run reports not just by account, but by *business perspective* (e.g., profitability by project, expenses by department).

- They remove the need for an excessively detailed chart of accounts. Instead of creating hundreds of accounts, you add dimensions as tags.

Examples of Dimensions

- **Department:** Finance, Sales, HR

- **Project:** Project A, Project B

- **Location:** Chennai, Bangalore

- **Customer Group:** Retail, Wholesale

Example in Action

- When recording travel expenses in a journal, the entry goes to "50100 – Travel Expenses."

- By tagging it with the dimension **Department = Sales**, management can later run a report showing *how much the sales team spent on travel this quarter.*

How Journals and Dimensions Work Together

Consider this scenario:

- An accountant records salary expenses for the month.

- Using the **General Journal**, they debit "Salary Expenses" and credit "Bank Account."

- At the same time, they assign the **Department dimension** (Finance, Sales, HR) to split the expenses.

When reports are generated:

- **Without Dimensions:** You only see the total salary expense.

- **With Dimensions:** You see salary expense broken down by department, helping managers make better decisions. This process is visually explained in Figure 2-4.

Real-Life Workflow Example

Scenario: Departmental Expense Allocation

1. Finance team receives office rental invoice for ₹1,00,000.

2. In the **General Journal**, they post it to the "Rent Expense" account.

3. To allocate the cost between departments, they enter two journal lines:

   - ₹40,000 with Department = Sales

   - ₹60,000 with Department = Operations

4. When posted, each line updates the G/L with its assigned dimension.

5. Management can then run a Profit and Loss by Department report to see rent consumption by each team.

Later, management runs a **P&L by Department** report, instantly seeing how much rent each team consumed.

Benefits

- **Accuracy:** Journals provide a controlled entry point for transactions.

- **Flexibility:** Dimensions let you analyze data without bloating the chart of accounts.

- **Transparency:** Reports can be filtered and grouped by business segments.

- **Efficiency:** Recurring journals save time for monthly or repetitive postings.

Common Challenges

- **Forgetting to Assign Dimensions:** Incomplete analysis in reports

- **Overusing Too Many Dimensions:** Complexity without added value

- **Incorrect Setup of Journals:** Misclassification of entries

Best Practices

- Keep the number of dimensions meaningful (two to four core dimensions).

- Use **default dimensions** for customers, vendors, items, or G/L accounts to reduce manual tagging.

- Review journal batches regularly before posting.

- Train users to understand why dimensions matter, not just how to enter them.

Accounting Transaction Process

Figure 2-4. *Accounting transaction process: a step-by-step flow in Business Central showing how journal entries are recorded, dimensions added, entries posted, and reports generated for analysis*

An example of journal entries with and without dimensions is shown in Table 2-4.

Table 2-4. *Journal entries recorded with and without dimensions in Business Central*

Date	Document No.	G/L Account	Description	Debit (₹)	Credit (₹)	Dimension (Without)	Dimension (With)
01-08-2025	INV-001	50100	Travel expenses	10,000		–	Department = Sales
01-08-2025	INV-001	20100	Vendor payables		10,000	–	Department = Sales
05-08-2025	JV-002	50200	Office supplies	5,000		–	Department = HR
05-08-2025	JV-002	10100	Bank account		5,000	–	Department = HR
10-08-2025	JV-003	60100	Rent expense	1,00,000		–	Sales = 40, Operations = 60
10-08-2025	JV-003	20100	Vendor payables		1,00,000	–	Sales = 40, Operations = 60

Journals and dimensions are the practical tools that turn Business Central into more than just an accounting system. Journals ensure that transactions are posted correctly and securely, while dimensions allow businesses to view their data from multiple angles. By mastering these, organizations can go beyond bookkeeping and unlock powerful insights for better decision-making.

Document Approvals

In any organization, not every transaction can or should be posted directly. To maintain control, prevent fraud, and ensure compliance, approvals are built into the workflow. Business Central provides a flexible **document approval system** that allows companies to enforce checks before important records, like purchase orders, sales invoices, or journal entries, are finalized.

With approvals in place, a junior employee can create a document, but only a manager or designated approver can authorize it. This ensures accuracy, accountability, and financial discipline across the organization.

Tip   Integrate approvals with **Outlook or Teams notifications** so approvers don't miss requests.

What Can Be Approved?

Business Central allows approval workflows for various documents and processes:

- **Sales Documents:** Quotes, orders, invoices, credit memos

- **Purchase Documents:** Requisitions, orders, invoices

- **Payment Journals:** Outgoing payments requiring the finance manager's sign-off

- **General Journals:** Adjustments and accruals that need senior approval

- **Timesheets and Expense Reports:** For employee and project tracking

Approval Workflow Basics

Approval workflows in Business Central are built around three main elements:

1. **Requester:** Creates the document (e.g., a purchase order)

2. **Approver:** Reviews and either approves or rejects the request

3. **Workflow Rules:** Define who approves what, based on thresholds (e.g., purchases above ₹50,000 must be approved by the Finance Head)

Process Flow

Requester creates document ➤ Workflow triggered ➤ Approver notified (via BC, email, or Teams) ➤ Approver approves/rejects ➤ Document status updated ➤ Only approved documents can be posted. The approval timeline in Business Central is depicted in Figure 2-5.

Example: Purchase Order Approval

Scenario

- A purchasing officer raises a purchase order for office furniture worth ₹75,000.

- The company's approval rule is

  - **Purchases up to ₹50,000:** Department Manager

  - **Purchases Above ₹50,000:** Finance Director

Steps

1. Officer creates the purchase order.

2. The system checks the threshold and, if the Approver Type is set to *First Qualified Approver*, routes the document to the Finance Director.

3. The Finance Director receives a notification inside Business Central (and optionally in Outlook/Teams).

4. After reviewing, the director approves.

5. The purchase order is released and ready for posting.

If rejected, the document is sent back with comments, preventing accidental or unauthorized posting.

Benefits of Approval Workflows

- **Control:** Prevents unauthorized spending or posting.

- **Accountability:** Clear record of who approved what and when.

- **Transparency:** Audit trail for compliance and financial review.

- **Efficiency:** Automated notifications reduce delays and paperwork.

- **Flexibility:** Approvals can be single-level or multilevel, depending on company policy.

Common Challenges

- Overly complex approval chains can slow down business.

- If rules aren't reviewed regularly, thresholds may become outdated.

- Users may try to bypass approvals if the process feels too rigid.

Best Practices

- Keep approval hierarchies simple and practical.

- Set realistic thresholds (e.g., low-value purchases should not require senior approval).

- Integrate with **email/Teams notifications** to avoid bottlenecks.

- Regularly audit approval logs to check compliance.

Real-Life Use Case

Case: A mid-sized manufacturing firm uses approvals for purchase invoices.

- Any invoice above ₹1,00,000 must be approved by the CFO.

- An invoice for raw materials worth ₹1,20,000 is entered by Accounts Payable.

- The workflow routes it to the CFO ➤ CFO reviews supplier terms and budget ➤ Approves.

- The invoice is posted, and the liability reflects in the G/L.

This ensures the company does not commit to large expenses without senior oversight.

Examples of approval rules are summarized in Table 2-5.

Table 2-5. *Common approval rules for purchase, sales, and journal documents*

Document Type	Condition/ Threshold	Approver Role	Purpose
Purchase Order	Up to ₹50,000	Department Manager	Ensures routine purchases are monitored at the departmental level.
Purchase Order	Above ₹50,000	Finance Director	Provides control over high-value commitments.
Sales Discount	Discount greater than 10%	Sales Manager	Prevents excessive discounts that affect margins.
Purchase Invoice	Above ₹1,00,000	CFO	Senior-level oversight for significant expenses.
Payment Journal	Any vendor payment > ₹5,00,000	Finance Head	Protects cash flow by requiring approval for large payouts.
General Journal	Manual adjustments above ₹25,000	Chief Accountant	Controls nonstandard entries in the general ledger.
Expense Claim	Any claim above ₹10,000	HR Manager	Ensures employee expenses are reasonable and verified.

Document Approval Process Timeline

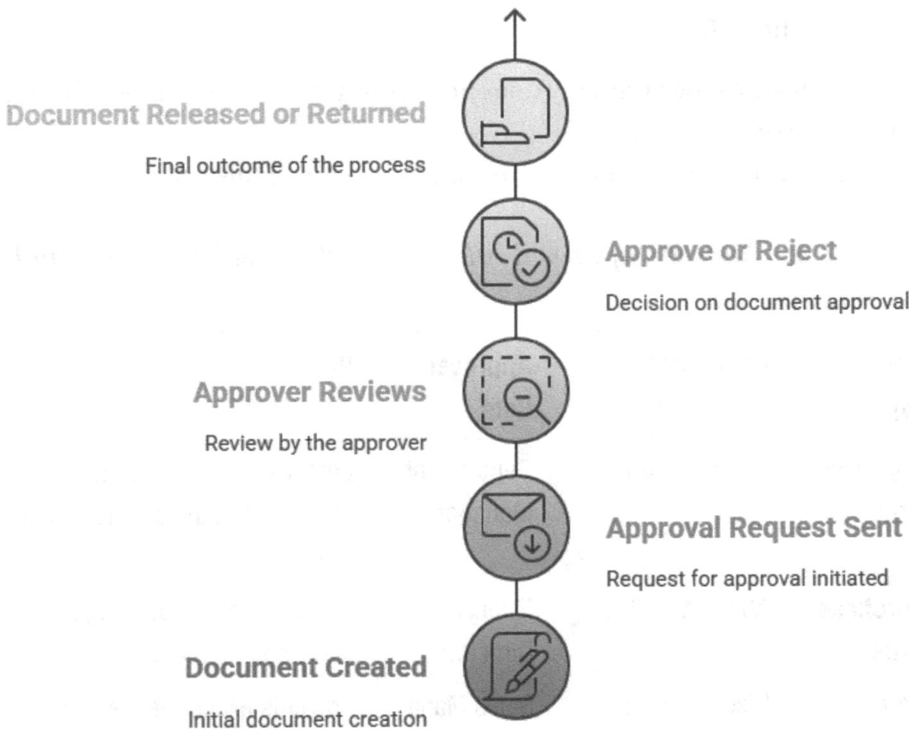

Figure 2-5. *Document approval process timeline: from document creation to final release or return, Business Central manages approvals through request submission, approver review, and approve/reject decisions*

Approvals in Business Central provide a structured way to enforce internal controls and protect company resources. By implementing approval workflows for critical documents, organizations can balance speed with accountability, ensuring that every transaction is authorized and traceable.

Conclusion

The functional essentials of Business Central provide the backbone for how organizations manage their daily financial and operational activities. Starting with the **chart of accounts and posting groups**, we saw how financial data is structured and automatically mapped to the right accounts. The **sales and purchase cycles** demonstrated how customer and vendor processes mirror each other, ensuring smooth order-to-cash and procure-to-pay flows. With **journals and dimensions**, Business Central offers flexible ways to record transactions and enrich them with business context for deeper analysis. Finally, **document approvals** enforce control and accountability, ensuring that only authorized transactions are processed.

Mastering these fundamentals is critical. They not only help you run day-to-day operations efficiently but also provide a solid foundation for advanced features such as reporting, automation, and integration. In short, these essentials form the language of Business Central that every functional consultant and user must be fluent in.

Chapter Highlights

- **Chart of Accounts and Posting Groups:** Define structure and rules for accurate financial postings.

- **Sales Cycle:** Covers quote, order, shipment, invoice, and payment to manage customer transactions.

- **Purchase Cycle:** Covers quote, order, receipt, invoice, and payment to manage vendor transactions.

- **Journals:** Safe staging areas for transactions like payments, adjustments, or inventory updates.

- **Dimensions:** Analytical tags that provide insights by department, project, or location.

- **Document Approvals:** Workflows that maintain control, transparency, and compliance.

- **Key Learning:** These processes link finance, operations, and reporting, forming the core of Business Central's functional capability.

Self-Check Questions

Chart of Accounts and Posting Groups

1. What is the difference between a chart of accounts and posting groups?

2. Give an example of how a Customer Posting Group works when a sales invoice is posted.

3. Why should businesses avoid creating too many accounts in the chart of accounts?

Sales and Purchase Cycle

1. List the five key steps in the sales cycle.

2. How does the purchase cycle mirror the sales cycle? Give one example.

3. What happens in Business Central when you post a Purchase Receipt?

Journals and Dimensions

1. What is the purpose of using journals instead of directly editing the G/L?

2. Name three types of journals and their typical use.

3. How do dimensions help reduce the need for an overly detailed chart of accounts?

Document Approvals

1. Why are approval workflows important in Business Central?

2. Give an example of an approval rule for a purchase order.

3. What happens if an approver rejects a document in the workflow?

Suggested Answers and Hints

Chart of Accounts and Posting Groups

1. **Difference**

   - **Chart of Accounts:** A structured list of all G/L accounts used to record transactions

   - **Posting Groups:** Rules that automatically direct transactions to the correct G/L accounts

2. **Example**

- When posting a sales invoice for a domestic customer, the **Customer Posting Group** routes the receivable to *20100 – Trade Receivables (Domestic)* instead of requiring the user to choose it manually.

3. **Too Many Accounts?**

- It complicates maintenance and reporting. Instead of creating separate accounts for every detail, businesses should use **dimensions** for analysis.

Sales and Purchase Cycle

1. **Sales Cycle Steps:** Quote ➤ Order ➤ Shipment ➤ Invoice ➤ Payment

2. **Mirror Structure**

- Sales cycle ends with customer payment (cash in).

- Purchase cycle ends with vendor payment (cash out).

- Example: *Sales Order = Purchase Order, Sales Invoice = Purchase Invoice.*

3. **Posting a Purchase Receipt**

- Increases inventory (asset) in the G/L

- Creates item ledger entries

- Does not create a vendor liability until the invoice is posted

Journals and Dimensions

1. **Purpose of Journals**

   - Safe workspace to record, review, and batch transactions before they update the G/L. Helps prevent errors.

2. **Types of Journals**

   - **General Journal:** Corrections, accruals, allocations.

   - **Payment Journal:** Outgoing vendor payments.

   - **Item Journal:** Adjust inventory quantities or costs.

3. **Dimensions vs. Detailed COA**

   - Instead of creating 20 expense accounts for each department, you can have 1 "Travel Expense" account and use **Department dimensions** to split costs.

Document Approvals

1. **Why Approvals Matter**

   - They prevent unauthorized transactions, ensure compliance, and provide an audit trail.

2. **Example Approval Rule**

   - Any *purchase order* above ₹50,000 must be approved by the Finance Director.

3. **Rejection Effect**

    - The document is returned to the requester with status "Rejected." It cannot be posted until corrected and resubmitted.

Practical Exercises

Exercise 1: Chart of Accounts and Posting Groups

- Create three new G/L accounts:

    - **70200:** Training Expenses

    - **70300:** Marketing Expenses

    - **70400:** Consultancy Fees

- Assign appropriate **Vendor Posting Groups** so that when you post a vendor invoice, expenses automatically hit the correct account.

- Post a test vendor invoice of ₹20,000 for "Consultancy Fees" and verify the G/L entry.

Exercise 2: Sales Cycle Simulation

- Create a **sales quote** for a customer who wants ten laptops.

- Convert the quote to a **sales order**.

- Post a **shipment** of the laptops.

- Post a **sales invoice** for the order.

- Record the **customer payment** and check the effect on the Bank and Receivables accounts.

Exercise 3: Purchase Cycle Simulation

- Request a **purchase quote** from a vendor for 50 office chairs.

- Convert it into a **purchase order**.

- Post a **receipt** of the chairs into inventory.

- Enter the **vendor invoice**.

- Make the **vendor payment** and confirm that the Bank and Payables accounts are updated.

Exercise 4: Journals and Dimensions

- Open a **General Journal** and record an office rent expense of ₹1,00,000.

- Assign **Dimensions:** Sales Department (40%), Operations Department (60%).

- Post the entry and run a **Profit and Loss by Department** report to see the breakdown.

- Repeat the same entry **without dimensions** and compare the reporting difference.

Exercise 5: Document Approvals

- Configure an approval workflow:

  - **Purchases up to ₹50,000:** Department Manager approval

  - **Purchases above ₹50,000:** Finance Director approval

- Create a **purchase order** worth ₹75,000.

- Submit it for approval and track the workflow notification.

- Approve the document and post it.

CHAPTER 3

Technical Essentials: AL and Extensions

In this chapter, we move from understanding Business Central as a user to exploring it as a developer. Business Central runs on a programming language called **AL (Application Language)**, and every customization is delivered as an **extension**. This approach makes it possible to adapt the system to unique business needs without altering the standard application.

The chapter begins with the **AL development environment**, how to set it up, how the project files are arranged, and what role each file plays. Once the environment is ready, we focus on the two most common customization needs: extending **tables** to add new data and extending **pages** to adjust how information is displayed to users.

After this, we introduce **events and triggers**, which are essential for creating flexible solutions. Instead of changing the base code, developers can subscribe to system events and write their own logic that runs at the right time. This way, the customizations remain upgrade-safe and easier to maintain.

Finally, the chapter covers **Visual Studio Code configuration**. Since VS Code is the main tool for AL development, learning how to organize the workspace, use extensions, and apply shortcuts will save time and improve efficiency.

© Dr. Gomathi S 2025

Dr. Gomathi S, *Microsoft Dynamics 365 Business Central Essentials*, Apress Pocket Guides, https://doi.org/10.1007/979-8-8688-2229-2_3

By the end of this chapter, readers will have a strong foundation in AL development. They will know how to

- Prepare and understand the AL project structure.

- Create simple table and page extensions.

- Use events and triggers to add business logic.

- Configure VS Code for smoother development.

This chapter is designed to make the first step into AL development approachable. It balances technical explanations with practical guidance, ensuring that readers can start writing their own customizations with confidence.

AL Setup and File Structure

Before writing any AL code, it is important to prepare the development environment. Business Central uses **Visual Studio Code (VS Code)** as its editor, and developers connect it to a Business Central sandbox to test and deploy their work.

Setting Up the Environment

1. **Install Visual Studio Code**

   Visual Studio Code is a free and lightweight editor available from Microsoft. It is the official tool for AL development. Once installed, it becomes the central workspace where all coding and extension management take place.

2. **Add the AL Language Extension**

   Microsoft provides an AL Language extension that
   integrates directly into VS Code. This extension includes
   syntax highlighting, IntelliSense, debugging support,
   and project templates. After installation, it becomes
   possible to create new AL projects from VS Code itself.

3. **Connect to a Business Central Sandbox**

   A sandbox environment is required to test and
   publish extensions. Developers use a Microsoft 365
   account with access to Business Central. By pressing
   AL: Go! in VS Code, a connection is established
   between the editor and the sandbox. This step also
   downloads symbols from the environment, allowing
   developers to reference standard Business Central
   objects in their code.

Understanding the AL Project Structure

When you create a new AL project, VS Code generates a set of files and
folders. Each has a specific role in building the extension:

- **app.json**

  This is the heart of the project. It contains metadata
  such as the extension name, publisher, version, and
  dependencies. Business Central uses this file to identify
  and manage the extension.

- **launch.json**

  The *launch.json* file specifies how VS Code connects to
  the target environment for publishing or debugging an
  extension. It includes settings such as the server URL,

authentication method, startup object, and schema update mode. Developers can use this configuration to deploy and debug the extension directly from VS Code.

- **AL Files (.al)**

  These are the source code files where tables, pages, reports, and other objects are written. Each object type has its own structure and properties.

  For example, a *table.al* file defines new tables or fields, and when you need to add fields to an existing standard table, you use a *tableextension.al* file; similarly, a *pageextension.al* file customizes user interface pages.

- **.vscode Folder**

  This hidden folder holds project-specific settings for VS Code. It ensures that debugging and publishing behave consistently across different developers working on the same project.

- **Translations Folder (optional)**

  If the extension supports multiple languages, translation files are stored here. These files allow field captions, labels, and messages to be localized.

File Naming and Organization

A good file structure makes projects easier to maintain. Some common practices include

- Naming files clearly, such as CustomerTableExt.al or SalesOrderPage.PageExt.al, so their purpose is obvious.

- Grouping related objects into folders (e.g., Tables, Pages, Codeunits).

- Maintaining consistency across the project so future developers can navigate it easily.

System Requirements and Prerequisites

Before starting AL development in Business Central, certain system and account requirements must be in place. These ensure that your setup works smoothly without unexpected errors.

1. **Minimum Requirements for Running VS Code and Business Central Sandbox**

   - **Visual Studio Code (VS Code):** You need the latest version of VS Code, which is free and lightweight.

   - **Operating System:** Works on Windows, macOS, and Linux.

   - **Hardware:** At least 4 GB RAM (8 GB recommended) and a stable internet connection.

   - **Sandbox Environment:** A Business Central sandbox is required to test and publish your extensions. The sandbox acts like a safe playground where you can experiment without affecting production data.

Tip   Always develop and test in a sandbox environment before moving to production.

---

2. **Role of Microsoft 365 Tenant and BC License (Trial vs. Production)**

   - **Microsoft 365 Tenant:** A tenant (your organization's Microsoft account) is needed to access Business Central. Without this, you cannot connect VS Code to a sandbox.

   - **Business Central License**

     - **Trial License:** Provides temporary access for learning and testing. Ideal for new developers or proof-of-concept projects.

     - **Production License:** Required for real-world business use. Production licenses ensure you can deploy extensions to live environments.

Important   Even if you use a trial license for practice, the extension you build works the same way as in production.

---

3. **Browser Requirements (Edge/Chrome)**

   - Business Central runs entirely in a web browser. For best performance and compatibility, use **Microsoft Edge** or **Google Chrome**.

   - In addition to Microsoft Edge and Google Chrome for Windows, Business Central is also designed to work with the current version of Mozilla Firefox for Windows and Safari for macOS.

Tip   Keep your browser updated to avoid issues with page rendering or missing features.

Steps to Download Symbols

Before writing AL code, developers need to download **symbols** from the Business Central environment.

1. **What Are Symbols?**

   - Symbols are the **metadata of standard Business Central objects** (like tables, pages, codeunits, and enums).

   - They act as a reference library so that your AL project recognizes existing objects and their properties.

   - Without symbols, VS Code will not understand objects such as *Customer Table* or *Sales Order Page*.

Important   Think of symbols as the "dictionary" that tells VS Code what each Business Central object means.

2. **How to Download Symbols**

   - Open **Visual Studio Code**.

   - Press **Ctrl+Shift+P** to open the Command Palette.

   - Type and select **AL: Download Symbols**.

- VS Code connects to your Business Central sandbox and downloads all metadata files.

- Once complete, you can see and use standard Business Central objects in your project.

Tip   If symbol download fails, check your sandbox connection settings in *launch.json*.

---

3. **Why This Is Mandatory Before Writing Extensions**

   - Without symbols, your AL project will not compile because it cannot "see" the standard objects.

   - Downloading symbols ensures that

     - You can extend existing objects (e.g., add fields to the Customer table).

     - IntelliSense works in VS Code (auto-suggestions for fields, methods, and triggers).

     - Your code remains aligned with the version of Business Central in your sandbox.

Understanding the app.json in Detail

- Explain each important property:

  - **id:** Unique GUID

  - **name:** Extension name

  - **publisher:** Company or developer

- **version:** Extension versioning

- **platform & application:** Compatibility with BC versions

- **dependencies:** When an extension relies on another app

Debugging Basics

Debugging is an essential step in AL development. It helps developers test their code, identify errors, and ensure the extension works as expected.

1. **How launch.json Supports Debugging**

   - The **launch.json** file contains all the details required to connect VS Code with the Business Central sandbox.

   - It specifies the server URL, authentication method, and startup object (the page or table that should open when debugging begins).

   - When you press **F5** in VS Code, the editor uses the active configuration in launch.json to publish the extension to the selected environment and then launch it in debug mode.

2. **Difference Between Publish, Publish Without Debugging, and Publish with Debugging**

   - **Publish with Debugging (F5):** The extension is published to the target environment, and the debugger is attached, allowing you to step through code.

- **Publish Without Debugging (Ctrl+F5):** The extension is published, but the debugger is not attached; use this for faster testing of functionality.

- **Debug Without Publishing (Ctrl+Shift+F5):** The debugger is attached to the last published version of your extension or to base app code, without re-publishing.

- **Other Publish Commands:** In recent versions of the AL extension or via the Command Palette, you may also find options like "Publish and open in Designer" or "Publish full dependent tree" for more advanced deployment scopes.

3. **How Breakpoints Can Be Added in AL Files**

- Open any .al file in VS Code.

- Click to the left of the code line number, or press **F9**, to set a **breakpoint**.

- When the debugger runs, execution will pause at that line. You can then inspect variable values, check conditions, and step through the code line by line.

- Breakpoints can also be toggled on or off as needed.

Typical Project Layout Example

Show a small **screenshot or a text diagram** of how the folder structure looks:

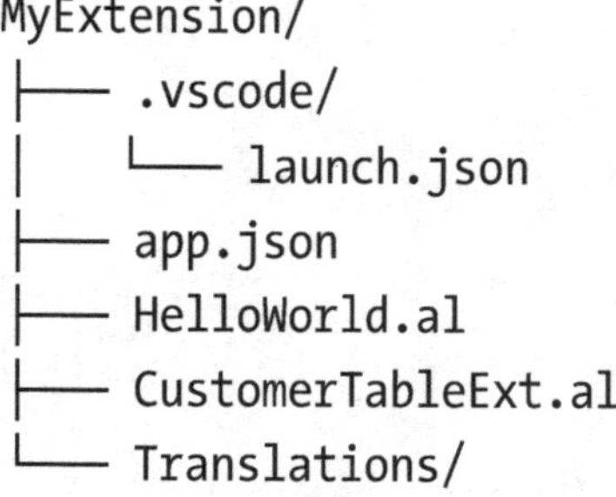

```
MyExtension/
├── .vscode/
│   └── launch.json
├── app.json
├── HelloWorld.al
├── CustomerTableExt.al
└── Translations/
```

Visual learners understand better with this.

Best Practices for File Structure

- Use separate folders (Tables, Pages, Codeunits).

- Use a **registered three-character prefix or suffix** for all object names (e.g., "*ABC_CustomerExt*"). This affix must be registered under your publisher name and ensures unique naming when your extension is published to AppSource.

- Keep file names aligned with object names.

Hands-On Mini Exercise

- Example: "Create a new project and add a single AL file that shows a Hello World message."

- This helps break the theory with something practical.

Common Errors in Setup

- Symbol download failure

- Authentication errors with sandbox

- Wrong version in app.json

Once the setup is complete and the project files are created, the developer can try adding a simple AL file. For example, creating a table extension that adds a custom field to the **Customer** table.

After publishing the extension to the sandbox, the new field exists in the table and is ready for use; however, to show the field on existing pages, such as the Customer Card, you also need to create a page extension that adds the field control to the page layout. This small exercise helps new developers see how each part of the setup comes together.

Important   Before writing extensions, download the symbols from the sandbox. Without symbols, VS Code cannot recognize standard Business Central objects.

VS Code Configuration

Developing AL extensions in Business Central begins with **Visual Studio Code (VS Code)**. It is not just a text editor; it becomes a full development environment once properly configured. Microsoft chose VS Code because it is cross-platform, lightweight, and easily customizable with extensions.

Correct configuration ensures that developers can write code, connect to Business Central environments, debug extensions, and collaborate effectively. As shown in Figure 3-1, every AL project includes key configuration files such as app.json and launch.json, which define the extension's identity and environment deployment settings. Additional files like rad.json and snapshots.json are generated by the system to support rapid-application-development workflows but are not meant to be modified manually.

Core Configuration Files

Every AL project created in VS Code has a set of configuration files that define how the extension works and how it connects to Business Central. The three most important ones are

1. **app.json**

2. **launch.json**

3. **rad.json**

Let us explore each in detail.

Core Configuration Files in VS Code for AL Projects

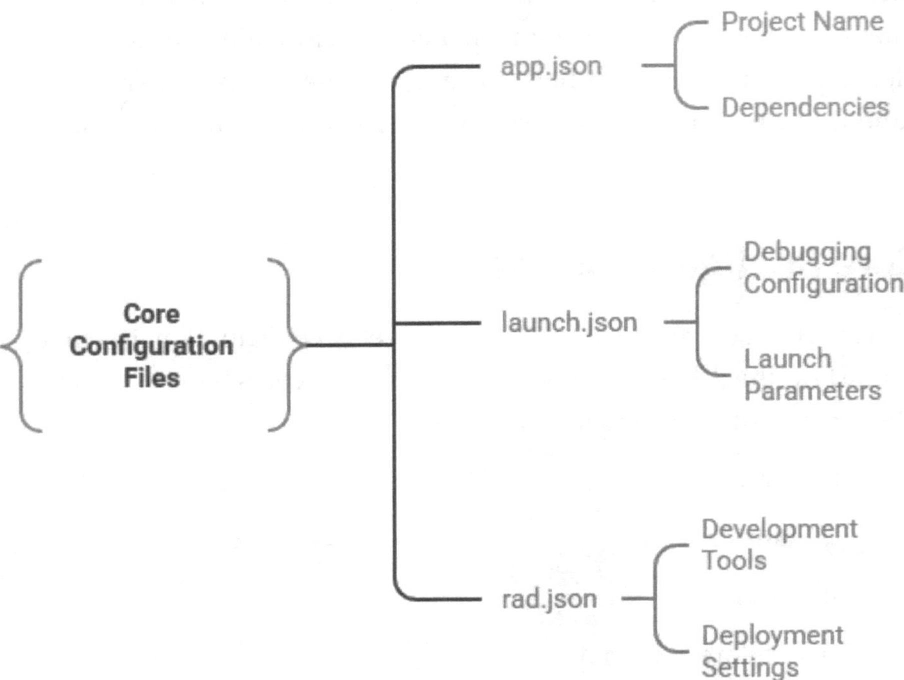

Figure 3-1. *Core configuration files in VS Code for AL projects*

app.json

This file defines the **identity** and **dependencies** of the extension. It tells Business Central what the extension is, who published it, and which version it belongs to.

Key Properties in app.json

- **id:** A unique GUID that identifies the extension

- **name:** The extension's name

- **publisher:** The developer or company publishing the app

- **version:** The version number of the extension (e.g., 1.0.0.0)

- **platform:** The minimum platform version required

- **application:** The Business Central version compatibility

- **dependencies:** Lists other extensions that this one depends on

Example

```json
{

    "id": "f2c1d6e0-7f7a-4c28-b02e-5d9f7e7f4c12",
    "name": "Company Asset Management",
    "publisher": "Contoso Solutions",
    "version": "1.0.0.0",
    "platform": "25.0.0.0",
    "application": "25.0.0.0",
    "dependencies": []
}
```

Think of app.json as the **extension's passport**. It carries its identity and compatibility information.

launch.json

This file is stored inside the .vscode folder. It controls how VS Code **publishes and debugs** the extension in Business Central.

Key Properties in launch.json

- **server:** The Business Central environment URL

- **serverInstance:** Instance name (e.g., Sandbox)

- **authentication:** Authentication method (UserPassword, AAD)

- **startupObjectId:** Object (table, page) to open when debugging starts

- **schemaUpdateMode:** Defines whether schema changes are synchronized

Example

```json
{
    "version": "0.2.0",
    "configurations": [
        {
            "name": "Sandbox",
            "type": "al",
            "request": "launch",
            "server": "https://businesscentral.dynamics.com",
            "serverInstance": "Sandbox",
            "authentication": "UserPassword",
            "startupObjectId": 50100,
            "schemaUpdateMode": "Synchronize"
        }
    ]
}
```

Think of launch.json as the **bridge** between VS Code and your Business Central environment.

rad.json

The *rad.json* file is part of the RAD (Rapid Application Development) workflow in Business Central and is automatically generated in your project's *.vscode* folder. It tracks changes between builds for incremental publishing (RAD publishing). It is **not** intended as a configuration file to be manually edited or committed to source control.

Purpose of rad.json

- Tracks changes to application objects (tables, pages, codeunits, profiles) between builds, enabling incremental (RAD) publishing for faster deployment in development workflows.

- Is automatically generated, maintained, and cleared by the AL tooling; it is not intended to be edited manually or used as an environment-profiles file.

- Does not include unchanged files such as translation files, permission sets, custom report layouts, or table data during RAD publishing.

Example rad.json:

```
{
    "environments": [
        {
            "name": "Sandbox-Dev",
            "tenant": "default",
            "server": "https://businesscentral.dynamics.com",
            "environmentType": "Sandbox",
            "applicationFamily": "BusinessCentral"
        },
```

```
        {
            "name": "Production",
            "tenant": "default",
            "server": "https://businesscentral.dynamics.com",
            "environmentType": "Production",
            "applicationFamily": "BusinessCentral"
        }
    ],
    "settings": {
        "showMyCode": true,
        "resourceExposurePolicy": {
            "allowDebugging": true,
            "allowDownloadingSource": true,
            "includeSourceInSymbolFile": true
        }
    }
}
```

Explanation

- This rad.json defines two environments: a Sandbox for development and a Production environment.

- Developers can switch easily between them without rewriting configurations.

- It also defines policies like allowing debugging and source downloading.

Think of rad.json as the **environment manager** for your project.

Recommended VS Code Extensions for AL Developers

Besides Microsoft's AL Language extension, the following are highly recommended:

- **AL Object Designer:** Browse Business Central objects visually.

- **AZ AL Dev Tools:** Renumber objects, generate symbols, manage IDs.

- **GitLens:** Version control with Git, track changes.

- **AL Code Outline:** Quick navigation inside AL files.

Keyboard Shortcuts Worth Remembering

- **Ctrl+Shift+P:** Open Command Palette (run AL commands).

- **F5:** Publish and debug the extension.

- **Alt+Up/Down:** Move lines of code.

- **Ctrl+/:** Comment/uncomment code.

- **Ctrl+K Z:** Zen mode for distraction-free coding.

Organizing the Workspace

Whether you are working in a single AL project (one folder) or using a multi-root workspace for multiple projects, good organization helps reduce confusion and improve collaboration.

- **Use Separate Folders:** Within your project, structure folders logically (e.g., *Tables, Pages, Codeunits, Reports*).

- **Naming Conventions:** Use filenames that align with object names (e.g., *AssetTable.al, AssetListPage.al*).

- **Version Control:** Connect your project to a repository (e.g., GitHub, Azure DevOps) to track code changes and support team collaboration.

If you are working on multiple extensions or dependent projects at once, you can use a VS Code workspace (with multiple folders) so you can open, build, and manage them together.

Debugging in VS Code

Debugging helps developers step through code and analyze issues.

- Set breakpoints in .al files.

- Use F5 to run in debug mode.

- Inspect variables and call stacks in the debug console.

For example, if a trigger is misbehaving, breakpoints help identify exactly where the logic runs.

Proper configuration of VS Code is the foundation of AL development.

- **app.json** defines the extension's identity.

- **launch.json** controls publishing and debugging.

- *rad.json* is a temporary system-generated file used by the Rapid Application Development (RAD) feature to track changed objects between builds. It enables faster incremental publishing during development but is automatically cleared when the extension is fully published.

Together, these files, along with a well-organized workspace, debugging setup, and productivity extensions, make VS Code a powerful and flexible tool for building Business Central extensions.

Introduction: Objects in Business Central

In Business Central, everything that a developer creates or customizes is built as an **object**. Objects are the building blocks of the system. They define how data is stored, how it is displayed to users, and how business logic is executed.

What Are Objects?

An **object** is a defined piece of functionality written in AL. It can be a table that stores data, a page that displays information, or a report that presents data in a specific format. By combining different object types, developers shape the way Business Central behaves for end users. As shown in Figure 3-2, Business Central relies on different types of objects, each serving a specific purpose. Tables store business data, pages provide user interaction, reports process and display information, while codeunits, queries, XMLPorts, enums, and profiles extend functionality and user experience.

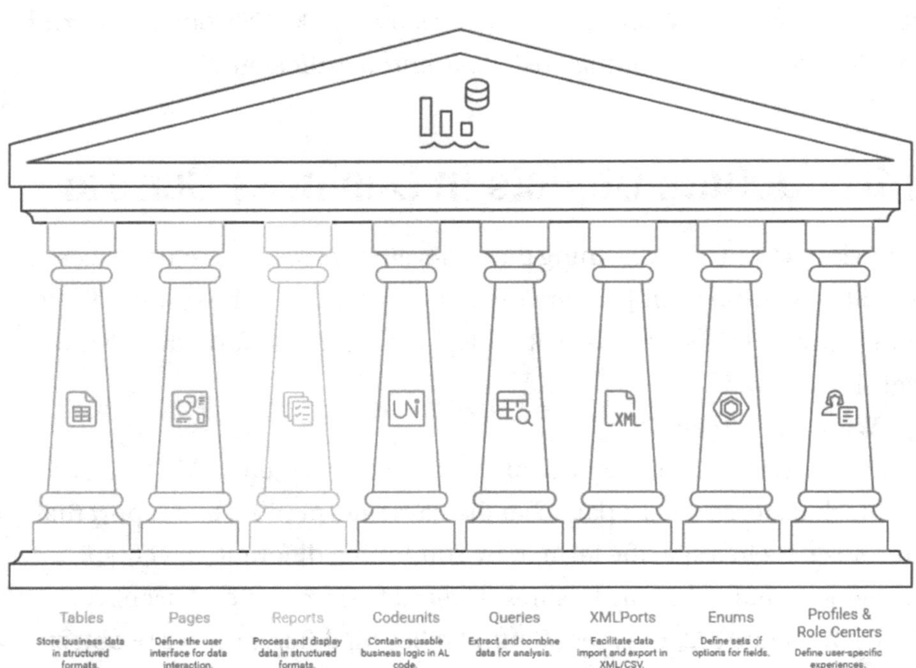

Figure 3-2. *Business Central objects and their roles*

Types of Objects in Business Central

1. **Tables**

   - Store business data (e.g., customers, vendors, items, sales orders).

   - Contain fields (columns) and records (rows).

   - Example: The **Item table** stores product details like Item No., Description, and Unit Price.

2. **Pages**

   - Define the user interface (UI) of Business Central.

   - Allow users to view and interact with data stored in tables.

   - Example: The **Customer Card page** lets users edit customer information.

3. **Reports**

   - Process and display data in structured formats such as PDF or Excel.

   - Can be used for invoices, statements, or analytical summaries.

   - Example: A **Sales Invoice report** generates customer invoices.

4. **Codeunits**

   - Contain AL code that groups business logic into reusable units.

   - Used for complex calculations, posting routines, or validations.

   - Example: A **posting codeunit** handles the process of posting sales orders to the ledger.

5. **Queries**

   - Extract and combine data from multiple tables for analysis or reports.

   - Similar to SQL queries but written in AL syntax.

   - Example: A query that joins Customers and Sales Orders to analyze sales by region.

6. **XMLPorts**

   - Used for importing and exporting data in XML or CSV format.

   - Example: Importing vendor price lists from an external system.

7. **Enums**

   - Define sets of options that can be used in fields.

   - Example: A Payment Method enum might include values like Cash, Bank Transfer, and Card.

8. **Profiles and Role Centers**

   - Define the layout and role-specific experience of users.

   - Example: A **Sales Role Center** dashboard showing KPIs, sales orders, and shortcuts.

Why Objects Matter

Understanding objects is fundamental because every customization in Business Central is either

- Creating a **new object** or

- Extending an **existing object**

When developers use VS Code with AL, they are essentially writing and managing these objects. Each object type serves a unique purpose, but together, they create the full ERP experience, data storage, business rules, and user interaction. Refer to Table 3-1 to see how different Business Central objects contribute to development. Each object type has a distinct role: tables for storing data, pages for user interaction, reports for presenting information, and codeunits, queries, XMLPorts, enums, and profiles for extending system behavior and user experience.

Table 3-1. *Types of objects in Business Central*

Object Type	Purpose	Example
Table	Stores business data in structured fields and records	Customer table (stores customer details)
Page	Provides a user interface to view, enter, or edit data	Customer Card page (displays one customer)
Report	Processes data and outputs it in formats like PDF or Excel	Sales Invoice report
Codeunit	Groups AL code for business logic and processes	Posting routines for sales orders
Query	Retrieves and combines data from multiple tables	Sales by Region query
XMLPort	Imports or exports data in XML/CSV formats	Import vendor price list
Enum	Defines fixed option sets used in fields	Payment Method (Cash, Bank Transfer, Card)
Profile/Role Center	Defines role-specific UI and dashboards	Sales Role Center dashboard

As shown in Figure 3-3, Business Central development follows a structured flow. It begins with **Role Centers and Profiles**, which define the user experience, and then cascades down to **Pages** and **Tables** that manage how data is displayed and stored. From there, **Codeunits** handle the business logic, while **Reports** and **Queries** process and present data. Finally, **XMLPorts** and **Enums** extend integration and provide controlled option sets, completing the customization cycle.

Tip   When naming files, align them with object names (e.g., CustomerTableExt.al) to avoid confusion.

Business Central Development Flowchart

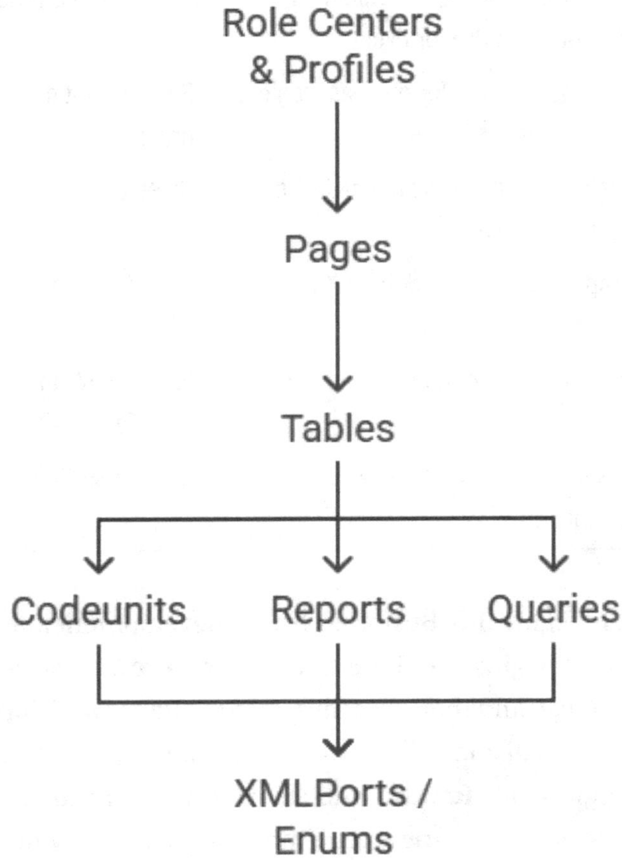

Figure 3-3. *Business Central development flowchart: showing the sequence from Role Centers and Profiles down to Pages, Tables, Codeunits, Reports, Queries, and finally XMLPorts/Enums*

Table and Page Extensions

Tables in Business Central

Tables are the backbone of Business Central. Every piece of business data, including customers, vendors, items, sales orders, or invoices, is stored in a table. Just like in a traditional database, tables consist of fields (such as Customer Name, Posting Date, or Amount) and records (the actual rows of data).

Without tables, the system would have no structure to store and retrieve information. For example:

- The **Customer table** keeps all customer records.

- The **Item table** holds product details.

- The **Sales Header and Sales Line tables** store sales orders.

In short, **tables define what data is stored and how it is organized.**

Suppose a company wants to maintain a list of company assets (like laptops, chairs, and projectors). While Business Central includes the standard **Fixed Asset** table (ID 5600) for full fixed-asset management tasks, you may choose to create a **custom asset table** if your use case is simpler or does not require full depreciation, ledger entries, or fixed-asset reporting functionality.

Note   The Company Asset table below is designed only for training purposes, to show how fields, keys, and properties are defined, and does not include the accounting or depreciation logic that exists in the standard Fixed Asset module.

```
table 50100 "Company Asset"
{
    DataClassification = ToBeClassified;

    fields
    {
        field(1; "Asset ID"; Code[20])
        {
            Caption = 'Asset ID';
        }
        field(2; "Asset Name"; Text[50])
        {
            Caption = 'Asset Name';
        }
        field(3; "Purchase Date"; Date)
        {
            Caption = 'Purchase Date';
        }
        field(4; "Cost"; Decimal)
        {
            Caption = 'Cost';
        }
    }

    keys
    {
        key(PK; "Asset ID")
        {
            Clustered = true;
        }
    }
}
```

- This creates a new table called Company Asset.

- It has fields for Asset ID, Asset Name, Purchase Date, and Cost.

- Asset ID is the primary key, which uniquely identifies each asset.

- Every time the company records a new asset, a row is added to this table.

Pages in Business Central

While tables manage data in the background, **pages are the user interface** through which users interact with that data. Pages present the fields from tables in a meaningful layout, making them easier to read, enter, and update.

For example:

- The **Customer Card page** displays a single customer's details.

- The **Sales Order page** allows users to create and post orders.

- The **Item List page** shows a list of products available.

Pages determine how data appears to users, what actions they can take, and how they navigate between related records.

In short, **tables store the data, and pages display the data**.

Why Do We Need Extensions?

Every business is unique. A standard Business Central installation may not cover all specific requirements. For example:

- A manufacturing company may want to track *Machine Serial Numbers* for each item.

- A trading firm may need a field for the *Import License Code* on vendor records.

- A retail company may want a shortcut action to view *Loyalty Points* directly on the Customer Card.

Instead of altering Microsoft's standard tables and pages, which would make future upgrades difficult, Business Central allows developers to create **extensions**. Extensions are safe, modular changes that enhance the system while keeping the base code intact.

Now that we have a table, users need a way to interact with it. We create a **List Page** to display all assets in a grid format.

```al
page 50100 "Company Asset List"
{
    PageType = List;
    SourceTable = "Company Asset";
    ApplicationArea = All;
    UsageCategory = Lists;

    layout
    {
        area(content)
        {
            repeater(Group)
            {
                field("Asset ID"; "Asset ID") { }
                field("Asset Name"; "Asset Name") { }
                field("Purchase Date"; "Purchase Date") { }
                field("Cost"; Cost) { }
```

```
        }
      }
    }
}
```

- This creates a List Page called Company Asset List.

- The SourceTable is Company Asset, meaning the page displays data stored in that table.

- The repeater section defines which fields appear in the list.

- Users can now add, edit, and view company assets directly from this page.

Table Extensions

A **table extension** is used when you need to add extra fields or properties to an existing table. It "extends" the functionality of the base table without replacing it.

- **When to Use**

  - When additional business-specific data must be stored

  - When you need to link new fields with reporting or processes

- **Example Use Case:** Adding a field called "GST Registration No." to the Customer table

Suppose a business needs to store the **GST Registration No.** for each customer, but the standard Customer table does not have this field.

```
tableextension 50100 CustomerExtension extends
Customer
{
    fields
    {
        field(50100; "GST Registration No.";
        Code[20])
        {
            Caption = 'GST Registration No.';
        }
    }
}
```

- This code extends the Customer table.

- It adds a new field called GST Registration No. with a length of 20 characters.

- The field becomes part of every customer record in the database, but it does not yet appear on the page.

Page Extensions

A **page extension** is used when you want to adjust how data appears to the user. This can include adding new fields (from a table extension), rearranging sections, or adding actions such as buttons and menus.

- **When to Use**

  - When new fields must be made visible to users

  - When the layout of a page needs improvement

  - When you want to add extra actions for convenience

- **Example Use Case:** Displaying the "GST Registration No." field on the Customer Card page.

```
pageextension 50101 CustomerCardExtension extends
"Customer Card"
{
    layout
    {
        addlast(General)
        {
            field("GST Registration No."; "GST
            Registration No.")
            {
                ApplicationArea = All;
            }
        }
    }
}
```

- This code extends the Customer Card page.

- It places the new field "GST Registration No." in the General section of the page.

- Users can now enter and update this value directly when editing a customer.

How They Work Together

Think of it like this:

- **Table Extension = Add the data storage.**

- **Page Extension = Show the data to the user.**

Both usually go hand in hand. If you add a field to a table but don't update the page, users won't see it. Similarly, you cannot show a field on a page if the table does not contain it.

Events and Triggers

One of the most important principles in Business Central development is **avoiding direct modification of the base application**. Instead of changing Microsoft's standard code, developers rely on **events and triggers** to insert their custom logic. This approach ensures that customizations remain safe during upgrades and do not break standard functionality.

What Are Triggers?

Triggers are built-in entry points inside AL objects (tables, pages, codeunits, etc.) that automatically run when specific actions occur. They can be thought of as "predefined hooks" provided by Business Central.

For example:

- In a **table**, triggers can run when a record is inserted, modified, or deleted.

- On a **page**, triggers can run when the page opens or when a field is validated.

Common Table Triggers

- **OnInsert():** Runs when a new record is added

- **OnModify():** Runs when an existing record is changed

- **OnDelete():** Runs when a record is removed

- **OnValidate(FieldName):** Runs when a field value is validated

Example: Using a Trigger in a Table

```
table 50100 "Company Asset"
{
    fields
    {
        field(1; "Asset ID"; Code[20]) { }
        field(2; "Asset Name"; Text[50]) { }
        field(3; "Cost"; Decimal) { }
    }
    trigger OnInsert()
    begin
        Message('A new asset record has been created: %1',
        "Asset Name");
    end;
}
```

Explanation

Here, whenever a new asset record is inserted, a message is displayed with the asset's name. This is a simple use of a trigger to give feedback or enforce business rules.

What Are Events?

Events are predefined points in the application where developers can "subscribe" and add their own logic without changing the original code. Events are like "signals" raised by the system or custom code, and **event subscribers** listen to these signals and perform actions.

- **Publisher:** The object that raises the event

- **Subscriber:** A method inside a codeunit that listens for the published event and executes custom logic when the event is raised

Types of Events

In AL development for Business Central, there are **four main types of events**:

1. **Trigger Events:** Automatically raised by the system at predefined points (e.g., when a record is inserted, modified, deleted, or validated). They are "before/after" events tied to a table or page trigger.

2. **Global Events:** Predefined system events raised by core objects (such as when a company opens or environment variables change).

3. **Business Events:** Custom events defined by ISVs or Microsoft that carry a formal contract and promise stability across releases (used for workflows, integration, external systems).

4. **Integration Events:** Custom events that enable integration but do not carry the same guarantee of stability; they allow other extensions or applications to hook into your logic without modifying base code.

Why Use Events Instead of Modifications?

- **Upgrade Safe:** Standard code is never touched, so Microsoft updates won't overwrite your logic.

- **Reusability:** Multiple subscribers can listen to the same event.

- **Flexibility:** Logic can be turned on/off by enabling or disabling extensions.

As shown in Table 3-2, triggers are useful when working within your own objects (e.g., validating data in a custom table), whereas events are best when extending standard processes without modifying Microsoft's base code. Using events ensures upgrade-safe development.

Table 3-2. *Difference between triggers and events*

Feature	Triggers	Events
Defined in	Inside the object (table, page)	Raised by the system or developer
Scope	Runs automatically in the object	Requires a subscriber to respond
Modification	Part of the object's definition	External, does not touch base object
Use Case	Record validation, table changes	Extend standard processes safely

Example: Event Subscription

Suppose we want to run some logic every time a new customer is created, without modifying the Customer table. We can subscribe to the OnAfterInsertEvent of the Customer table.

```
codeunit 50100 CustomerEventSubscriber
{
    [EventSubscriber(ObjectType::Table, Database::Customer,
    'OnAfterInsertEvent', '', false, false)]
    local procedure AfterCustomerInsert(var Rec: Record
    Customer)
    begin
        Message('Customer %1 has been created successfully.',
        Rec."No.");
    end;
}
```

Explanation

- This codeunit subscribes to the **OnAfterInsertEvent** of the Customer table.

- Each time a new customer is added, a message is shown.

- Notice that the Customer table itself is not modified; the logic is separate and safe.

When to Use Triggers vs. Events

- **Use Triggers** when you are creating your own new object (like a custom table) and want to control what happens during insert, modify, delete, or validation.

- **Use Events** when you want to add logic to **existing Business Central processes** (like posting sales, validating customers, or calculating inventory) without modifying the standard objects.

Events and triggers form the backbone of upgrade-safe development in Business Central.

- **Triggers** are built into objects and execute automatically when actions happen.

- **Events** allow developers to "plug in" their logic into standard processes through subscriptions.

Together, they enable developers to extend the application while keeping the standard system clean and future-proof.

Conclusion

This chapter introduced the essential building blocks of technical development in Business Central. Readers learned that all customizations are created through objects, and every extension relies on these objects to deliver business-specific functionality. By understanding how to set up AL projects in VS Code, configure project files like app.json, launch.json, and rad.json, and follow a structured file organization, developers can start building confidently.

We also explored how tables and pages form the foundation of Business Central and how extensions allow safe modifications without disrupting the standard application. Finally, we examined events and triggers, two core mechanisms that make customizations flexible, upgrade-safe, and maintainable.

By the end of this chapter, readers should feel comfortable setting up their AL environment, creating their first objects, and extending standard functionality in a clean, structured way.

Chapter Highlights

- **Objects are the foundation** of Business Central development; everything in AL is built on them.

- **AL setup and file structure:** VS Code, AL Language extension, and sandbox connection form the basic environment.

- **Configuration files:**

  - app.json defines extension identity and compatibility.

  - launch.json manages publishing and debugging.

- rad.json simplifies environment and deployment handling.

- **Tables** store data; **Pages** display and interact with data.

- **Table extensions** add new fields or properties; **Page extensions** make these fields visible to users.

- **Events and triggers** allow custom logic to run safely without modifying base code.

- **Triggers** are defined inside objects; **Events** are external and subscribed to by other objects.

- Upgrade-safe development is achieved by using **extensions, events, and proper VS Code setup.**

Self-Check Questions

1. **Objects in Business Central**

   - What are objects in Business Central, and why are they important for developers?

   - Name at least four different object types and give one example for each.

2. **AL Setup and File Structure**

   - What is the role of app.json in an AL project?

   - How is launch.json different from rad.json?

   - Why do developers need to download symbols before starting AL development?

3. **VS Code Configuration**

   - Which three files (app.json, launch.json, rad. json) are considered the backbone of project configuration, and what does each one control?

   - What is the difference between schemaUpdateMode = Synchronize and schemaUpdateMode = Recreate?

   - List two VS Code extensions that improve productivity for AL developers.

4. **Tables and Pages**

   - What is the difference between a **master table** and a **transaction table**?

   - How do **card pages** differ from **list pages**?

   - Why do developers prefer table and page extensions instead of modifying standard objects directly?

5. **Table and Page Extensions**

   - When should you create a new table vs. a table extension?

   - What is the purpose of a page extension, and how does it connect with a table extension?

6. **Events and Triggers**

   - What is a trigger, and give one example of where it is used.

   - What is an event, and how is it different from a trigger?

   - Why are event subscribers considered upgrade-safe?

7. **General Application**

- If a business wants to add a new field called "Warranty Expiry Date" for items, which objects (and which type of extension) would you create?

- Suppose a company wants to run custom logic whenever a sales order is posted. Would you use a trigger or an event? Why?

Suggested Answers

1. **Objects in Business Central**

- **Definition:** Objects are the building blocks of Business Central. They define how data is stored (tables), how it is displayed (pages), how it is processed (codeunits/reports), and how users interact with the system.

- **Examples:**

  - **Table:** Customer (stores customer records)

  - **Page:** Item Card (displays product details)

  - **Report:** Sales Invoice (prints invoices)

  - **Codeunit:** Sales-Post (business logic for posting sales orders)

2. **AL Setup and File Structure**

- **app.json:** Defines the extension's identity (ID, name, publisher, version) and compatibility with Business Central.

- **launch.json:** Controls publishing and debugging by linking VS Code to the sandbox environment.

- A temporary, system-generated file used by the Rapid Application Development (RAD) feature. It tracks object changes between builds to enable faster incremental publishing during development. It is automatically created, updated, and cleared when the extension is published.

- **Symbols:** They are metadata of standard BC objects. Downloading symbols is mandatory because it lets AL projects reference standard objects like Customer, Item, etc.

3. **VS Code Configuration**

   - **Three Backbone Files**

     - **app.json:** Identity and dependencies

     - **launch.json:** Debugging and publishing configuration

     - **rad.json:** Environment profiles and deployment settings

   - **Schema Update Mode**

     - **Synchronize:** Keeps existing data when updating schema

     - **Recreate:** Drops and recreates the table, erasing data

   - **Productivity Extensions**

     - AL Object Designer

     - AZ AL Dev Tools

     - GitLens (for version control)

4. **Tables and Pages**

- **Master vs. Transaction Table**

    - Master table stores reference data (e.g., Item, Customer).

    - Transaction table stores activity/entries (e.g., Sales Header, Purchase Line).

- **Card vs. List Page**

    - Card page shows one record at a time (e.g., Customer Card).

    - List page shows multiple records in a table view (e.g., Vendor List).

- **Why Extensions:** Extensions avoid modifying base objects, making the system upgrade-safe and maintainable.

5. **Table and Page Extensions**

- **New Table vs. Table Extension**

    - Create a new table when the data structure is completely new (e.g., Company Assets).

    - Use a table extension when adding extra fields to an existing standard table (e.g., add "GST Number" to Customer).

- **Purpose of Page Extension:** A page extension displays new fields added via table extensions or customizes layout and actions. It ensures users can see and work with the new data.

6. **Events and Triggers**

- **Trigger:** A built-in hook inside an object that runs automatically.

  Example: OnInsert() in a table runs when a new record is created.

- **Event:** A signal raised by the system or developer, to which code can subscribe.

  Example: OnAfterInsertEvent in the Customer table can be subscribed to in a codeunit.

- **Why Upgrade-Safe:** Event subscribers are external to the standard object, so they don't change Microsoft's base code and remain safe across updates.

7. **General Application**

- **Warranty Expiry Date Field**

  - Create a *table extension* on the Item table to store the new field.

  - Create a *page extension* on the Item Card page to display it to users.

- **Custom Logic on Sales Order Posting**

  - Use an **event subscription** (not a trigger), because posting is a standard process. Subscribing ensures the logic runs safely without modifying the core posting routine.

Practice Exercises

Exercise 1: AL Project Setup

1. Install **Visual Studio Code** and the **AL Language extension**.

2. Create a new AL project by running AL: Go! from the Command Palette.

3. Examine the generated files (app.json, launch.json, .vscode folder).

4. Download symbols from your sandbox environment.

5. Identify what each file does in your project.

Exercise 2: Working with Configuration Files

1. Open app.json and

   - Change the extension name to "My First Extension".

   - Update the publisher name to your initials or company name.

   - Increment the version from 1.0.0.0 to 1.0.0.1.

2. In launch.json:

   - Change the startup object to open the Item List (ID 31) when debugging.

   (Optional) Add another configuration block for a Production environment.

3. In rad.json:

- The rad.json file is automatically generated when using Rapid Application Development. It tracks changed objects for faster incremental publishing and should **not** be manually edited or used for environment profiles.

Exercise 3: Create a New Table and Page

1. Create a new table called **"Training Course"** with the following fields:

- Course ID (Code[20])

- Course Name (Text[100])

- Duration (Integer)

- Start Date (Date)

2. Create a **List Page** called "Training Course List" to display these fields.

3. Publish the extension and add at least two sample training courses.

Exercise 4: Table Extension and Page Extension

1. Extend the **Item table** by adding a new field called "Warranty Expiry Date" (Date).

2. Create a **page extension** on the **Item Card page** to display this new field under the "General" FastTab.

3. Publish the extension and test by adding warranty dates for a few items.

Exercise 5: Using Triggers

1. Add an OnInsert trigger to the **Training Course table** created in Exercise 3.

2. Display a message when a new course is added:

   "Course <Course Name> has been created successfully."

3. Test by creating a new training course.

Exercise 6: Subscribing to an Event

1. Create a new **codeunit** called CustomerEventSubscriber.

2. Subscribe to the **Customer.OnAfterInsertEvent**.

3. Display a message when a customer is created:

   "Welcome, <Customer Name> has been added."

4. Test by creating a new customer record.

Exercise 7: Debugging

1. Set a breakpoint inside the trigger you wrote in Exercise 5.

2. Insert a new Training Course and step through the code using VS Code's debugger.

3. Inspect the value of variables while debugging.

CHAPTER 4

Consultant Tips, Best Practices, and Career Guide

Being a Business Central consultant is more than learning features; it is about applying them in real business situations, guiding clients, and shaping a professional career. This chapter is written to give readers practical advice that goes beyond theory.

We begin by introducing the **different types of consultants** involved in a Business Central project. Understanding these roles, functional, technical, solution architect, support, and others, helps new consultants know where they fit and what skills they should build.

From there, the chapter moves into **real-world project scenarios**, such as Fit-Gap analysis, User Acceptance Testing (UAT), and deployment. These examples show what happens in practice and how consultants solve challenges with clients.

Next, we provide **important checklists** for both functional and technical consultants. These serve as quick guides that can be used before go-live, during testing, or while gathering requirements.

© Dr. Gomathi S 2025

Dr. Gomathi S, *Microsoft Dynamics 365 Business Central Essentials*, Apress Pocket Guides, https://doi.org/10.1007/979-8-8688-2229-2_4

For those aiming to prove their expertise, we cover the **certification road map**, focusing on MB-800 (functional) and MB-820 (technical). Readers will learn how these exams support their career growth and how to prepare effectively.

Finally, the chapter closes with **career tips for new consultants**. From building communication skills to staying updated with Microsoft technologies, these insights help readers grow not just as consultants but as trusted advisors to their clients.

By the end of this chapter, readers will have a complete picture of what it takes to succeed as a Business Central consultant, understanding roles, mastering best practices, and preparing for a rewarding career.

Types of Consultants in Business Central

Every Business Central project needs people with different skills to work together. No single consultant can handle everything alone. Some focus on business processes, others on coding, and some on overall design or training. Each role has its own importance, and understanding these roles helps new consultants see where they fit and how they can grow in their career. Table 4-1 highlights the key consultant roles in a Business Central project. Each role plays a distinct part in ensuring successful implementation, from functional and technical setup to project governance, support, and user adoption.

Table 4-1. *Roles of consultants in a Business Central project*

Type of Consultant	Role	Example in Practice
Functional Consultant	Focuses on business processes and system setup. Works with clients to understand requirements and configure BC without coding.	Sets up posting groups, workflows, and trains users on sales or purchase processes.
Technical Consultant	Handles customizations, coding, and integrations. Uses AL language and extensions to build what BC does not offer out of the box.	Creates a custom table for vehicle tracking or integrates BC with a payroll system.
Solution Architect	Designs the overall solution, ensuring the system fits business needs and connects with other Microsoft tools.	Plans an architecture where BC integrates with Power BI for reporting and Power Automate for workflows.
Project Manager	Manages timelines, scope, budgets, and delivery. Bridges communication between client and consultants.	Runs weekly project meetings, tracks risks, and ensures on-time go-live.
Support Consultant	Provides post-go-live support, troubleshooting, and user assistance.	Resolves posting errors or helps new users with journal entries.
Change Management/ Training Consultant	Focuses on user adoption and communication. Prepares manuals and conducts workshops.	Helps finance users understand their new chart of accounts compared to the old system.

In smaller projects, a consultant may take on multiple roles (e.g., one person could be both functional and support). In larger projects, roles are clearly separated to ensure deep expertise and smoother delivery.

Real-World Scenarios: Fit-Gap, UAT, and Deployment

Every Business Central project follows a journey before the system goes live. Among the most critical stages are **Fit-Gap analysis**, **User Acceptance Testing (UAT)**, and **Deployment**. These stages decide whether the project succeeds or struggles.

Not all consultants are equally involved at every stage. For example, **functional consultants** and **solution architects** take the lead during Fit-Gap. **Technical consultants** become more active when gaps require custom development. **Project managers** are always present to ensure timelines and scope are met. **Support consultants** usually step in after deployment, while change management consultants play a vital role in UAT and training.

Let's explore each stage, along with how consultants contribute.

Fit-Gap Analysis

What It Is

Fit-Gap analysis compares the client's business requirements with the standard features of Business Central. A "fit" means the system can handle the requirement as-is. A "gap" means either the process must be adjusted or the system customized.

Steps Involved

1. Gather business requirements through workshops and interviews.

2. Map each requirement against Business Central's capabilities.

3. Identify which needs can be handled with standard setup (Fit).

4. Document which needs require customization or process change (Gap).

5. Agree with stakeholders on which approach to take for each gap.

Consultants' Roles

- **Functional Consultant:** Leads requirement gathering, compares processes with BC features, and documents fits/gaps.

- **Technical Consultant:** Provides input on how gaps can be solved with custom development or integration.

- **Solution Architect:** Oversees the overall solution design, ensuring the right balance between configuration and customization.

- **Project Manager:** Facilitates workshops, ensures decisions are tracked, and aligns business priorities with timelines.

- **Change Management Consultant (optional):** Helps explain process changes to users if gaps require altering their ways of working.

Example

A client needs automatic calculation of delivery charges based on distance. Business Central does not have this feature by default.

- Functional consultant documents it as a gap.

- Technical consultant suggests creating a custom extension.

- Solution architect checks whether the proposed customization is upgrade-safe and follows Microsoft's extension best practices

- Project manager ensures the client signs off on the decision.

User Acceptance Testing (UAT)

What It Is

UAT is when business users test the system in a safe environment before go-live. The purpose is to confirm that Business Central works as expected and that users are comfortable using it.

Steps Involved

1. Prepare test scripts covering real-life business processes.

2. Train users on how to run the tests.

3. Users perform activities such as creating orders, posting invoices, and running reports.

4. Collect feedback, log issues, and resolve them.

5. Obtain formal sign-off from users before moving to deployment.

Consultants' Roles

- **Functional Consultant:** Creates test cases, guides users, and validates results.

- **Technical Consultant:** Fixes issues or enhancements identified during UAT.

- **Solution Architect:** Ensures changes align with overall design and don't break other parts of the system.

- **Project Manager:** Tracks issues, ensures deadlines are met, and facilitates communication.

- **Change Management/Training Consultant:** Prepares training sessions, manuals, and supports users during testing.

Example

During UAT, a finance manager tests vendor invoice posting. They discover that the approval workflow does not trigger correctly for invoices above ₹1,00,000.

- Functional consultant reviews the workflow configuration.

- Technical consultant checks if customization caused the issue.

- Solution architect ensures the fix doesn't affect other workflows.

- Project manager logs the issue and tracks it to closure.

Deployment

What It Is

Deployment is the stage where the system moves from the test environment into the live environment. This is when the business officially starts using Business Central for daily operations.

Steps Involved

1. Finalize master data and opening balances.

2. Prepare a cutover plan (switching from the old system to BC).

3. Migrate all pending transactions (open sales orders, purchase orders, etc.).

4. Move configurations and customizations into the production environment.

5. Go-live support: consultants stay available to resolve issues.

Consultants' Roles

- **Functional Consultant:** Validates migrated data (customers, vendors, items, balances). Supports users on day one.

- **Technical Consultant:** Handles data migration scripts, ensures extensions are deployed correctly, and resolves technical issues.

- **Solution Architect:** Oversees that the deployment matches the design and ensures all integrations (Power BI, Outlook, APIs) are working.

- **Project Manager:** Coordinates the cutover plan, manages risks, and ensures minimal disruption.

- **Support Consultant:** Begins post-go-live support, handling tickets and helping users.

- **Change Management Consultant:** Provides on-the-job guidance and ensures user adoption.

Example

On go-live day, all open sales orders are migrated into BC. The sales team starts posting transactions.

- Functional consultant validates whether invoices post correctly.

- Technical consultant fixes any failed data imports.

- Project manager ensures the business resumes smoothly.

- Support consultant sets up a helpdesk for user issues.

Fit-Gap Analysis: Aligns business needs with BC features. Functional consultants lead, with support from technical and architects.

UAT: Confirms the system is ready for real-world use. All roles work together, with functional and training consultants closest to users.

Deployment: Moves the project into live operations. Technicals ensure stability, functionals support users, and support consultants step in.

Together, these stages highlight how **different consultants contribute at different moments**, ensuring that Business Central not only works technically but also fits the client's business perfectly.

Important Checklists for Technical and Functional Consultants

Every Business Central consultant, whether functional or technical, needs a reliable checklist to avoid missing critical steps in an implementation. These checklists act like road maps, ensuring that the project runs smoothly and no detail is overlooked.

While both roles work toward the same goal, their focus areas are different. The **functional consultant** focuses on business processes, configuration, and user adoption. The **technical consultant** ensures that customizations, integrations, and system performance are in place.

Functional Consultant Checklist

Before Implementation

- Conduct requirement workshops with key business users.

- Prepare Fit-Gap analysis and get client sign-off.

- Define the chart of accounts (COA), posting groups, and dimensions.

- Document master data needs (customers, vendors, items, employees).

- Finalize approval workflows and security roles.

During Implementation

- Configure system settings (General Ledger setup, VAT/GST, currencies, payment terms).

- Set up posting groups (Customer, Vendor, Item, Bank).

- Configure workflows (e.g., purchase approval, sales order approval).

- Load sample data for testing (customers, vendors, inventory).

- Validate business processes (Sales Order ➤ Invoice ➤ Payment).

Before UAT/Go-Live

- Prepare UAT scenarios and test scripts with end users.

- Train business users and provide documentation.

- Verify opening balances and initial master data migration.

- Check financial reports (Trial Balance, P&L, Balance Sheet) for accuracy.

- Get UAT sign-off from all departments.

Post Go-Live

- Support end users with initial transactions.

- Validate daily operations (posting journals, sales, purchase).

- Track and resolve user-reported issues.

- Suggest improvements for process efficiency.

Technical Consultant Checklist

Before Implementation

- Set up Business Central environments (Sandbox, UAT, Production).

- Ensure AL development environment is configured (VS Code, extensions).

- Review Fit-Gap analysis for development requirements.

- Estimate effort for customizations and integrations.

- Define integration points (Power BI, Power Automate, third-party apps).

During Implementation

- Develop extensions for identified gaps (tables, pages, reports, APIs).

- Follow AL coding best practices and naming conventions.

- Conduct unit testing for each customization.

- Create data migration scripts (customers, vendors, items, balances).

- Test integrations (Outlook, Teams, Power Platform, external apps).

Before UAT/Go-Live

- Move extensions from sandbox to UAT environment.

- Perform system testing with sample data.

- Support functional consultants during UAT issue resolution.

- Prepare a rollback plan in case of deployment errors.

- Document technical solutions for handover.

Post Go-Live

- Deploy final extensions and confirm no errors in production.

- Monitor performance and system logs.

- Fix any data migration or posting issues.

- Support functional consultants with bug fixes.

- Plan for future upgrades and extension compatibility.

Combined Checklist (for Both Roles Together)

Since functional and technical consultants work hand-in-hand, here's a **quick combined view.** Table 4-2 shows how functional and technical consultants contribute at each project stage. While functional consultants focus on business processes, training, and user support, technical consultants ensure the system is technically sound, customized, and integrated with other solutions.

Table 4-2. *Functional vs. technical focus across project stages*

Stage	Functional Focus	Technical Focus
Requirement Gathering	Document processes, prepare Fit-Gap	Validate the feasibility of gaps
System Setup	Configure COA, posting groups, workflows	Prepare dev environment, plan integrations
Testing (UAT)	Prepare test cases, guide users	Fix bugs, support with customizations
Deployment	Validate data migration, support users	Deploy extensions, ensure system stability
Post Go-Live	Train and support end users	Monitor performance, fix technical issues

These checklists act as a **practical toolkit** for consultants. By following them, consultants reduce errors, improve user confidence, and ensure a smoother project journey.

Certification to AIM (MB-820, MB-800)

Certifications are an important step in the career path of every Business Central consultant. They do not just validate your knowledge but also give you an edge in the job market. Microsoft offers two key certifications for Business Central under the **AIM (Accelerate, Innovate, Move)** strategy:

- **MB-800: Microsoft Dynamics 365 Business Central Functional Consultant Associate**

- **MB-820: Microsoft Dynamics 365 Business Central Developer Associate**

Each certification is designed for a different type of consultant. Choosing the right one depends on your career path.

MB-800: Business Central Functional Consultant Associate

Who Should Take It

- Functional consultants

- Finance and operations professionals

- Business analysts who configure systems

Skills Measured

- Setting up Business Central (finance, sales, purchase, inventory)

- Configuring master data, posting groups, dimensions, and approvals

- Working with sales and purchase cycles

- Managing reporting and user security

- Supporting end users

Benefits

- Proves your ability to configure and deliver Business Central without coding

- Makes you job-ready for roles like Functional Consultant, Business Analyst, or Support Consultant

Preparation Road Map

- Learn fundamentals (finance, sales, purchase, inventory).

- Practice configurations in a sandbox environment.

- Review Microsoft Learn modules for MB-800.

- Attempt practice tests and mock exams.

MB-820: Business Central Developer Associate

Who Should Take It

- Technical consultants

- AL developers

- Professionals working with integrations and extensions

Skills Measured

- Writing AL code for tables, pages, reports, and codeunits

- Developing and publishing extensions

- Integrating with Power Platform, APIs, and Azure services

- Following coding best practices and ensuring performance

- Testing and debugging solutions

Benefits

- Proves your capability as a Business Central developer

- Opens doors to technical roles like Developer, Technical Consultant, or Solution Architect in the future

Preparation Road Map

- Learn AL programming basics.

- Practice creating tables, pages, and extensions in VS Code.

- Study Microsoft Learn content for MB-820.

- Work on small real-world projects (e.g., custom approval, custom reports).

- Attempt practice labs and sample exams.

Choosing Between MB-800 and MB-820

If you are...	Take this certification
Strong in finance, sales, and business processes	**MB-800**
Interested in coding, integrations, and extensions	**MB-820**
Starting your career and unsure	Begin with **MB-800** to build a foundation, then move to MB-820 if coding excites you

Certification Tips

- Start with **Microsoft Learn** (official modules are free and comprehensive).

- Use a **sandbox environment** to practice (real learning comes from doing).

- Form a **study group or join community forums** to discuss doubts.

- Attempt **mock exams** to get exam-day confidence.

- Remember: passing the exam is not the end; apply the knowledge in projects.

Career Tips for New BC Consultants

Starting a career as a Business Central consultant can feel both exciting and overwhelming. The opportunities are vast, but so are the expectations. Whether you are on the **functional** side (working with business processes) or the **technical** side (working with AL development and integrations), success depends on a mix of skills, habits, and mindset.

Here are some career tips every new consultant should follow:

Build Strong Foundations

- **Understand Business Basics:** Learn finance, sales, purchase, and inventory concepts. Even technical consultants need this understanding to create meaningful solutions.

- **Practice in a Sandbox:** Set up your own demo company in Business Central and experiment with features daily.

- **Don't Skip Documentation:** Get used to writing requirement notes, solution design, and process flows.

Learn Continuously

- Business Central is updated frequently by Microsoft. Stay updated through **release notes, blogs, and community sessions**.

- Follow **Microsoft Learn paths** for both functional and technical roles.

- Explore related tools; **Power BI, Power Automate, Teams, and Excel** integration give you an edge.

Develop Communication Skills

- Consultants act as a bridge between clients and technology. Clear communication is your biggest asset.

- Learn to **explain technical terms in business language** that clients understand.

- Practice **active listening**; sometimes the unspoken needs of a client matter more than the spoken ones.

Gain Real Project Experience

- Start with smaller tasks (data migration, configuration, testing support) to build confidence.

- Observe senior consultants and solution architects, how they handle clients, document requirements, and make decisions.

- Don't hesitate to ask questions. Early curiosity builds strong expertise later.

Build a Professional Network

- Join **Microsoft Communities** (MCT Lounge, MVP blogs, LinkedIn groups, local meetups).

- Share your learnings on LinkedIn or YouTube; it builds credibility.

- Participate in hackathons, community challenges, or open source contributions in AL.

Certifications As Milestones

- Start with **MB-800** (functional) or **MB-820** (technical) as your entry-level badge.

- Plan future certifications depending on your career path (Solution Architect, Power Platform, Data Analytics).

- Treat certifications as milestones, not the destination; real growth comes from applying the knowledge.

Adopt the Right Mindset

- **Be Problem-Solving Oriented:** Instead of saying "this can't be done," explore "how else can it be done?"

- **Be Adaptable:** Each client works differently; flexibility is key.

- **Think Long-Term:** Don't just focus on project delivery; focus on building trust with clients.

Career Growth Path

- **Year 1–2:** Junior Functional/Technical Consultant ➤ focus on learning basics, supporting projects

- **Year 3–5:** Senior Consultant ➤ lead small projects, guide juniors, specialize in industries

- **Year 5+:** Solution Architect/Project Manager ➤ design solutions, manage teams, drive strategy

By following these tips, new consultants can move from being beginners to trusted advisors. The goal is not just to "know Business Central" but to **deliver value to businesses and grow as professionals**.

Common Mistakes New Consultants Make (and How to Avoid Them)

When starting out, many new consultants focus only on learning the system and forget the practical side of consulting. Being aware of common mistakes helps you avoid them early and build a stronger reputation.

1. **Over-customizing Instead of Using Standard Features**

   - **Mistake:** Jumping to technical solutions when a business process can be solved using standard Business Central features.

   - **Example:** Writing custom code for approvals when BC already has built-in workflows.

   - **How to Avoid:** Always check whether the requirement can be achieved with out-of-the-box functionality before requesting a customization.

2. **Ignoring Documentation**

   - **Mistake:** Not recording requirements, decisions, or changes clearly.

   - **Example:** A client asks for a change, but without documentation, the team forgets what was agreed.

   - **How to Avoid:** Make documentation a daily habit. Even short notes save confusion later.

3. **Poor Communication with Clients**

   - **Mistake:** Using technical terms clients don't understand or not clarifying requirements properly.

   - **Example:** Telling a finance user about "AL code changes" instead of explaining "we'll add a small customization to handle your requirement."

   - **How to Avoid:** Use business language with clients and technical language with developers. Adjust your style to the audience.

4. **Not Testing Thoroughly Before UAT**

- **Mistake:** Handing over a half-checked system to end users.

- **Example:** Users find errors in simple postings during UAT because consultants didn't pre-test.

- **How to Avoid:** Consultants should always test their setups or customizations before involving end users.

5. **Relying Too Much on Seniors**

- **Mistake:** Always waiting for a senior consultant's approval or solution.

- **Example:** Asking for help on small configuration issues instead of exploring.

- **How to Avoid:** Be curious and try to solve issues independently first. Seniors will respect initiative.

Industry Focus and Specialization Advice

Business Central is a flexible ERP used by companies in many industries, including **manufacturing, distribution, retail, finance, service, and more**. As a new consultant, it is good to have a broad understanding of all modules. But over time, developing **specialization in a specific industry** will make you stand out in the job market.

Why Specialization Matters

- Clients often prefer consultants who understand their industry challenges.

- Specialized consultants can give faster, more relevant solutions.

- It helps you become the "go-to person" for certain industries, opening higher-level roles and opportunities.

Example Areas of Specialization

- **Manufacturing:** Production orders, BOM (Bill of Materials), capacity planning

- **Retail:** POS (Point of Sale) integration, discounts, customer loyalty programs

- **Distribution/Logistics:** Warehouse management, shipment tracking, route planning

- **Finance:** Advanced reporting, cost accounting, consolidations

- **Service Industry:** Service orders, contracts, resource management

Practical Tip

In the first two to three years of your career:

- Get exposure to different industries.

- Notice where your interest is strongest.

- Then focus on becoming an expert in that domain.

Example: A consultant who specializes in **manufacturing** can lead projects for factories, advise on best practices, and command higher value compared to a general consultant.

Soft Skills That Matter

Technical knowledge and system expertise are important, but what truly makes a consultant successful are the **soft skills**. These are the human skills that help you connect with clients, build trust, and work effectively in teams. Many projects succeed or fail not because of technology, but because of how well consultants manage people.

1. **Communication**

   - Speak clearly and adapt your language to the audience.

   - Use simple business terms with clients and technical terms with developers.

   - Always confirm understanding; repeat back requirements to ensure you captured them correctly.

2. **Presentation Skills**

   - As a consultant, you will often demonstrate Business Central to clients.

   - Practice showing features in a simple, story-like flow instead of clicking randomly.

   - Use visuals and examples from the client's business to keep them engaged.

3. **Client Handling**

   - Clients may sometimes be frustrated, especially during testing or go-live.

   - Stay calm, listen patiently, and provide solutions instead of excuses.

- Always maintain professionalism, even under pressure.

4. **Team Collaboration**

- You will work with functional, technical, and project managers.

- Respect other roles and share information openly.

- Be flexible; sometimes you may need to step out of your role to support the team.

5. **Negotiation and Conflict Management**

- Clients may demand features that are not practical or within scope.

- Learn to explain alternatives and guide them to realistic solutions.

- When conflicts arise, focus on solving the problem, not winning the argument.

Remember: Business Central is just software. What makes a consultant valuable is the ability to **understand people, explain clearly, and deliver solutions with confidence**.

A Day in the Life of a Consultant

Understanding theory is useful, but seeing what a consultant actually does in a typical day makes the role real. Here's a glimpse into how a day might look for both functional and technical consultants during an implementation project.

Functional Consultant's Day

- **Morning:** Meet the client's finance team for a workshop on purchase approvals. Gather requirements and document their current process.

- **Late Morning:** Configure approval workflows in the test environment. Test the setup with a few sample transactions.

- **Afternoon:** Conduct a short training session for end users on how to create sales invoices.

- **Evening:** Write up meeting notes, update the Fit-Gap document, and share with the project manager.

The functional consultant spends the day bridging **business needs and system configuration**.

Technical Consultant's Day

- **Morning:** Review a customization request raised during UAT. The client wants an additional field on the Sales Order page.

- **Late Morning:** Open Visual Studio Code and develop an AL extension to add the field. Test it in the sandbox environment.

- **Afternoon:** Join a call with the solution architect to discuss API integration between Business Central and a third-party payroll system.

- **Evening:** Deploy the tested extension to UAT and document the changes for handover.

The technical consultant spends the day working on **customizations, coding, and integrations**.

Shared Moments Across Roles

- Both consultants join the daily project status call led by the project manager.

- Both troubleshoot issues raised by users, though from different perspectives (business vs. technical).

- Both collaborate closely to ensure the client gets a working solution.

This balance of workshops, configuration, coding, testing, and client interaction defines the daily rhythm of a consultant. While tasks differ, the **common thread is solving problems and supporting the client's journey**.

Global Opportunities for Business Central Consultants

One of the biggest advantages of becoming a Business Central consultant is the **global demand** for your skills. Business Central is used by small, medium, and large companies across industries and countries. Because it is a cloud-first ERP, many projects can be done remotely, while others offer opportunities for international travel and on-site consulting.

Why Global Opportunities Exist

- **Microsoft Ecosystem:** Business Central is tightly integrated with Microsoft 365, Power Platform, and Azure, all of which are used worldwide.

- **Cloud Adoption:** As more companies move from legacy systems to the cloud, they need skilled consultants to guide migrations.

- **Shortage of Experts:** There are fewer certified BC consultants compared to demand, making skilled professionals highly valued.

Remote and Onsite Roles

- Many consultants work fully **remote**, supporting clients across continents.

- Others travel onsite for workshops, go-lives, and training.

- Hybrid models are common, remote configuration with short onsite visits.

Career Expansion Paths

- Start as a **local consultant** ➤ move to **global projects** through Microsoft partners.

- Work with **international clients** to gain exposure to different business cultures and industries.

- Build expertise in **multi-currency, multi-language, and multi-legal environments**, which makes you globally competitive.

Example

A consultant in India may implement Business Central for a retail company in the UK, then support a manufacturing client in the United States, all without leaving their home country. Conversely, experienced consultants may be sent on-site for three to six months to guide large-scale deployments.

The bottom line: **Business Central skills travel with you.** Once you master the system, your opportunities are not limited to one country or industry; you can truly work anywhere in the world.

Conclusion

Being a Business Central consultant is not just about knowing the system; it's about applying it to solve real business problems and guiding clients with confidence. In this chapter, we explored the practical side of consulting, from understanding the different types of consultants to seeing how they contribute during Fit-Gap analysis, UAT, and deployment.

We also looked at ready-to-use **checklists** that ensure nothing important is missed during implementations, and we walked through the **certification road map (MB-800 and MB-820)** to help readers choose the right career track. Finally, we discussed **career tips for new consultants**, covering skills, mistakes to avoid, industry specialization, soft skills, daily life examples, and global opportunities.

Together, these insights form a strong foundation for anyone starting or advancing their career as a Business Central consultant. The message is clear: success comes from a balance of **technical knowledge, business understanding, soft skills, and continuous learning**.

Chapter Highlights

- Business Central projects involve different types of consultants: functional, technical, solution architects, project managers, support, and change management specialists.

- Real-world stages, **Fit-Gap analysis, UAT, and deployment**, show how consultants play different roles in ensuring project success.

- Functional and technical consultants rely on **checklists** to cover all tasks from requirement gathering to go-live and support.

- **MB-800 certification** is for functional consultants, while **MB-820 certification** is for technical consultants; both are key milestones in a consultant's career.

- New consultants should focus on

  - Building strong foundations in BC and business processes

  - Avoiding common mistakes like over-customization and poor documentation

  - Developing soft skills such as communication, presentation, and negotiation

  - Exploring **industry specialization** to stand out in the market

  - Embracing **global opportunities**, as BC consultants are in demand worldwide

- A consultant's growth path can lead from junior consultant ➤ senior consultant ➤ solution architect or project manager.

Self-Check Questions

1. **Types of Consultants**

   1. What is the main difference between a functional consultant and a technical consultant?

   2. Which consultant is responsible for the overall solution design in a project?

2. **Real-World Scenarios**

   1. What is Fit-Gap analysis, and why is it important?

   2. During UAT, who is mainly responsible for preparing test cases and guiding users?

   3. What are the key activities that happen during deployment?

3. **Checklists**

   1. Name two important tasks a functional consultant must complete before UAT.

   2. What should a technical consultant do before moving extensions to the production environment?

4. **Certifications**

   1. Which certification is best suited for a consultant who focuses on finance and business processes?

   2. Which certification proves skills in AL development and extensions?

5. **Career Tips**

   1. List two common mistakes new consultants make and how to avoid them.

   2. Why is industry specialization important for consultants?

   3. What are two soft skills that help consultants succeed?

6. **Growth and Opportunities**

   1. Describe one typical activity from the daily life of a functional consultant.

   2. Why do Business Central consultants have global opportunities?

Answers to Self-Check Questions

1. **Types of Consultants**

   - **Q:** What is the main difference between a functional consultant and a technical consultant?

     A: A functional consultant focuses on business processes and system configuration without coding, while a technical consultant works on customizations, AL development, and integrations.

   - **Q:** Which consultant is responsible for the overall solution design in a project?

     A: The Solution Architect.

2. **Real-World Scenarios**

   - **Q:** What is Fit-Gap analysis, and why is it important?

     A: Fit-Gap analysis compares business requirements with Business Central's standard features to identify what fits and where gaps exist. It ensures proper planning and reduces surprises later.

   - **Q:** During UAT, who is mainly responsible for preparing test cases and guiding users?

     A: The Functional Consultant.

   - **Q:** What are the key activities that happen during deployment?

     A: Migrating data, moving extensions to production, validating configurations, switching from the old system to Business Central, and providing go-live support.

3. **Checklists**

- **Q:** Name two important tasks a functional consultant must complete before UAT.

  A: Preparing UAT scenarios/test scripts and verifying opening balances/data migration.

- **Q:** What should a technical consultant do before moving extensions to the production environment?

  A: Perform system testing in UAT, ensure code quality, and prepare a rollback plan in case of issues.

4. **Certifications**

- **Q:** Which certification is best suited for a consultant who focuses on finance and business processes?

  A: MB-800: Business Central Functional Consultant Associate.

- **Q:** Which certification proves skills in AL development and extensions?

  A: MB-820: Business Central Developer Associate.

5. **Career Tips**

- **Q:** List two common mistakes new consultants make and how to avoid them.

  A: Over-customizing instead of using standard features (avoid by exploring built-in options first) and ignoring documentation (avoid by making documentation a daily habit).

- **Q:** Why is industry specialization important for consultants?

  A: It makes consultants more valuable by helping them provide faster, industry-specific solutions and stand out in the job market.

- **Q:** What are two soft skills that help consultants succeed?

  A: Communication and presentation skills (others include negotiation, client handling, and teamwork).

6. **Growth and Opportunities**

- **Q:** Describe one typical activity from the daily life of a functional consultant.

  A: Conducting a workshop with clients to gather requirements, then configuring workflows or posting groups in Business Central.

- **Q:** Why do Business Central consultants have global opportunities?

  A: Because Business Central is a cloud-first ERP used worldwide, and skilled consultants can support clients remotely or on-site across different countries and industries.

Practice Exercises

Exercise 1: Fit-Gap Analysis

You are working with a client who wants

1. Automatic approval for purchase invoices below ₹50,000

2. A customized field for "Delivery Location" on the Sales Order page

3. A dashboard in Power BI to view daily sales

   - Identify which requirements are **fits** (standard Business Central features) and which are **gaps** (require customization).

   - Suggest how each gap should be handled (customization, integration, or process change).

Exercise 2: UAT Planning

Prepare a **UAT checklist** for the following client processes:

- Creating and posting a sales order

- Approving a purchase invoice

- Posting a general journal

- Running a trial balance report

List the test steps, expected results, and who should test each scenario (user role).

Exercise 3: Deployment Cutover Plan

Your client is moving from an old accounting system to Business Central. Write down the steps you will include in the **cutover plan**, covering

- Data migration (customers, vendors, balances)

- Pending transactions (open sales orders, purchase orders)

- Configurations (posting groups, dimensions)

- Go-live support activities

Exercise 4: Consultant Role Mapping

For each of the following project activities, assign the right consultant type:

1. Writing AL code for a custom report

2. Conducting a workshop with finance users

3. Designing overall architecture with Power BI and Power Automate integration

4. Preparing the project timeline and ensuring milestones are achieved

5. Providing post-go-live support for end users

Match them with Functional Consultant, Technical Consultant, Solution Architect, Project Manager, and Support Consultant.

Exercise 5: Career Road Map

Imagine you are a **new BC consultant** starting today.

- Which certification will you attempt first (MB-800 or MB-820)? Why?

- Which industry would you like to specialize in (finance, retail, manufacturing, distribution, or service)?

- Write a **two-year career plan:** What skills, projects, and certifications will you focus on?

ANNEXURE 1

Business Central Keyboard Shortcuts

Business Central has a wide range of keyboard shortcuts that improve speed and efficiency. Instead of clicking through menus, these shortcuts let you quickly search, filter, navigate, and enter data.

To make it easy, the shortcuts are grouped into **Navigation**, **Filtering and Searching**, **Data Entry**, **Page and View Controls**, and **Other Useful Shortcuts**. Each table includes the shortcut, its action, and a simple explanation.

Navigation Shortcuts

Shortcut	Action	Explanation
F6	Next FastTab	Moves to the next FastTab section.
Shift+F6	Previous FastTab	Moves back to the earlier FastTab.
Alt+F6	Collapse Current FastTab	Collapses the FastTab you are on.
Shift+F12	Role Explorer	Opens Role Explorer to browse features.
Ctrl+F12	Switch Slim/Wide Page	Toggles between compact and wide page view.
Ctrl+Shift+F12	Focus Mode On/Off	Maximizes workspace by hiding menus.
Alt+Shift+W	Pop Out Page	Opens the page in a new window.

© Dr. Gomathi S 2025
Dr. Gomathi S, *Microsoft Dynamics 365 Business Central Essentials*, Apress Pocket Guides,
https://doi.org/10.1007/979-8-8688-2229-2

Filtering and Searching Shortcuts

Shortcut	Action	Explanation
Alt+Q	Tell Me/Search	Opens the Tell Me box to search for pages and data.
Ctrl+Alt+Q	Find Entries	Finds related entries for a record.
F3	Search	Activates search on the current page.
Alt+F3	Filter to This Field	Filters the list by the selected field's value.
Shift+Alt+F3	Filter to This Field	Alternative way to filter a field.
Ctrl+Alt+Shift+F3	Reset All Filters	Clears all filters at once.
Shift+F3	Toggle Filter Pane	Opens/closes filter pane.
Ctrl+Shift+F3	Toggle Filter Pane (Totals)	Focuses filter pane on totals.
Alt+F7	Sort by Current Column	Sorts list data by the column you are in.

Data Entry Shortcuts

Shortcut	Action	Explanation
Ctrl+Insert	Add New Line	Creates a new line in a list or journal.
Ctrl+Delete	Delete Line Item	Deletes the selected line.
Enter	Next QuickEntry	Moves to the next QuickEntry field.
Shift+Enter	Previous QuickEntry	Moves back to the previous QuickEntry.
Ctrl+Enter	Exit List/Next Field Outside List	Jumps out of the list or moves to the next field.
Ctrl+Shift+Enter	Next QuickEntry After List	Continues QuickEntry after a list ends.
F8	Copy from Cell Above	Copies value from the line above (useful in journals).

Page and View Controls

Shortcut	Action	Explanation
Ctrl+F5	Reload Business Central	Reloads the entire application.
F5	Refresh Data	Updates the page data quickly.
Shift+F10	Content Menu	Displays right-click menu for items.
Alt+Up Arrow	Show Tool Tip	Displays a tool tip or error message.
Alt+Down Arrow	Open Drop-Down	Opens drop-down options for a field.
Ctrl+Alt+Down Arrow	Show Details	Expands details for lookup pages.

Help and Support Shortcuts

Shortcut	Action	Explanation
Ctrl+F1	Business Central Help	Opens Help for the current context.
Ctrl+Shift+F1	Help and Support Page	Directs to support resources.
Alt+F2	Business Central Help	Alternative help shortcut.
Ctrl+Alt+F1	Inspect Page and Data	Opens inspection tool to check page fields, tables, and extensions.

Other Useful Shortcuts

Shortcut	Action	Explanation
Alt+N	New	Creates a new record/document.
Alt+Shift+N	OK and New	Saves and opens a fresh new record.
Alt+O	Add Note	Adds a note to a record.
Alt+T	My Settings	Opens the My Settings page.
Ctrl+Shift+Alt+C	Company Badge	Displays company badge.
Alt	Show Action Shortcuts	Displays shortcut letters for available actions.

Glossary of Key Terms

When working with Business Central, consultants, developers, and even end users often come across terms that may sound confusing at first. This glossary is designed to give quick and simple definitions with practical examples. It covers both **functional concepts** (used in day-to-day business processes) and **technical concepts** (used in customization and development).

Functional Terms in Business Central

Term	Definition	Example/Use Case
Chart of Accounts (COA)	Complete list of general ledger accounts used to classify all transactions.	GL accounts like *Sales*, *Bank Charges*, and *Salaries* are part of the COA.
Posting Groups	Rules that define how transactions are automatically posted to the right GL accounts.	*Customer Posting Group* links domestic customers to the *Domestic Sales Account*.
Dimensions	Tags to categorize and analyze transactions (e.g., department, project).	Expense tagged with *Department = Finance* for cost tracking.

(continued)

© Dr. Gomathi S 2025

Dr. Gomathi S, *Microsoft Dynamics 365 Business Central Essentials*, Apress Pocket Guides,
https://doi.org/10.1007/979-8-8688-2229-2

Term	Definition	Example/Use Case
Ledger Entries	The final posted records that reflect in accounts.	Posting an invoice creates *Customer Ledger Entry* and *GL Entry*.
General Ledger (GL)	The central accounting record containing all financial transactions.	End-of-year P&L is derived from the GL.
Subledger (Subsidiary Ledger)	Detailed record linked to the GL for specific accounts.	*Customer Ledger* shows invoices and payments for each customer.
Trial Balance	A report that lists all GL accounts with debit/credit totals to check balance accuracy.	Used monthly to verify books before financial close.
Balance Sheet	A financial statement showing assets, liabilities, and equity.	*Assets = Liabilities + Equity* is validated from this report.
Income Statement (P&L)	Shows revenues and expenses over a period to calculate profit/loss.	Monthly sales and expense data produce the P&L statement.
Bank Reconciliation	The process of matching system bank entries with actual bank statements.	Ensures Business Central's cash account equals the bank's record.
Customer Card	A master record storing customer details.	Contains fields like *Name, Address, Credit Limit, and Payment Terms*.
Vendor Card	A master record storing vendor (supplier) details.	Stores *Bank Account No., Payment Terms, and Vendor Posting Group*.

(*continued*)

Term	Definition	Example/Use Case
Item Card	Stores product or service details.	An item can be *Finished Goods, Raw Materials, or Services.*
Sales Order	A document to manage and track customer product/service orders.	Posting a sales order creates invoices and shipment records.
Purchase Order	A document to track goods/services ordered from vendors.	Posting a purchase order creates receipts and vendor invoices.
Journals	Worksheets to manually enter financial transactions before posting.	*General Journal* for adjusting entries; *Payment Journal* for vendor payments.
Document Approvals	Workflow that requires documents (like sales orders) to be approved before posting.	A manager approves a purchase order above ₹50,000.
VAT/GST Posting	Tax handling setup in BC that automatically calculates and posts tax entries.	A sales invoice applies GST of 18% and posts to the tax account.
Inventory Valuation	Determines how stock is valued in financial records.	Methods: FIFO, Average Cost, Standard Cost.
Fixed Assets	Records for company-owned long-term assets.	*Company Car* or *Machinery* tracked with depreciation schedules.
Cash Flow Forecast	A projection of expected income and expenses.	Helps management see cash shortages or surpluses.

Technical Terms in Business Central

Term	Definition	Example/Use Case
Tables	Core objects that store data in structured fields.	*Item Table* stores product details like name, price, and inventory.
Pages	User interface objects that display and manage data from tables.	*Sales Order Page* shows order header and line details.
Codeunits	Collections of AL code containing business logic or functions.	*Codeunit 80 (Sales-Post)* handles posting of sales orders.
Reports	Objects that process data and generate layouts for printing or analysis.	*Sales Invoice Report* prints invoices for customers.
XMLPorts	Objects for importing and exporting structured data (XML, CSV).	Importing a *Vendor Price List* from Excel using XMLPort.
Queries	Objects that extract and combine data from multiple tables.	A query pulling *Customer Name* and *Outstanding Balance*.
Enums	Lists of fixed options used as field values.	Payment Terms Enum: *COD, Net 30, Net 60*.
Extensions	Packages that add or modify functionality without touching the base app.	A *Payroll Extension* adds custom HR features.
Events	Triggers raised by the system or custom code to extend functionality.	*OnBeforeSalesPost* event lets you add validations before posting sales.
Event Subscribers	AL methods that listen and respond to events.	A subscriber that auto-updates a field when a customer record changes.

(*continued*)

Term	Definition	Example/Use Case
Triggers	System-defined code that executes on table/page actions.	*OnInsert* trigger validates data before inserting it into a table.
AL Language	The programming language used to develop Business Central extensions.	Writing AL code in Visual Studio Code to create a custom page.
RAD.json	A project configuration file with runtime settings, dependencies, and metadata.	Defines *application version* and *publisher* for an extension.
App.json	File that defines app identity, dependencies, and target platform in an AL project.	Specifies *name, publisher, and runtime version* for your extension.
Symbols	Metadata from base application objects, used for referencing in custom code.	Accessing fields from *Customer Table* by loading symbols.
Profiles (Role Centers)	Define the default layout and menus for specific user roles.	*Accountant Role Center* shows finance-related tiles.
Permissions/ Permission Sets	Define what a user can view, edit, or post.	*D365 BUS FULL ACCESS* gives access to all functional areas.
API Pages	Pages designed specifically for data integration through APIs.	*Customer API Page* used to integrate BC with an ecommerce app.
Connectors (Integration)	Prebuilt connections to external services like Power BI and Dataverse.	Using the *BC Connector in Power Automate* to trigger workflows.

(continued)

Term	Definition	Example/Use Case
Telemetry	Logging and monitoring feature for tracking performance and errors.	Collecting *telemetry signals in Azure Application Insights*.
Debugging	Tracing AL code execution to fix errors.	Setting breakpoints in VS Code to debug a posting routine.

Deployment Checklist

A deployment in Business Central is more than just publishing an extension or switching on a configuration. A well-planned deployment ensures that data, code, users, and integrations are aligned and that the system works as expected without disrupting daily business operations. This checklist helps consultants and project teams reduce risks and deliver smooth go-lives.

Pre-deployment Checks

Area	Checklist Item	Why It Matters
Environment Readiness	Confirm sandbox and production environments are set up and accessible.	Ensures correct target environment is used for deployment.
Backup	Take full backup of production database and configurations.	Provides recovery point in case of failure.
Extension Versioning	Verify app.json and dependencies are updated correctly.	Prevents version mismatch or missing symbols.
Code Review	Ensure AL code follows best practices (naming, performance, security).	Avoids technical debt and unexpected errors.
Test Coverage	All test cases executed in sandbox/ UAT and signed off by users.	Reduces risk of undiscovered issues.

(continued)

© Dr. Gomathi S 2025

Dr. Gomathi S, *Microsoft Dynamics 365 Business Central Essentials,* Apress Pocket Guides,
https://doi.org/10.1007/979-8-8688-2229-2

Area	Checklist Item	Why It Matters
Data Migration	Trial migration done and validated for completeness and accuracy.	Ensures clean and correct data in live system.
Integration Validation	Confirm external connections (APIs, Power BI, Dataverse) work in test.	Prevents disruptions in linked applications.
User Roles and Permissions	Verify permission sets are assigned correctly.	Avoids business disruption due to access issues.
Communication Plan	Notify stakeholders of downtime, deployment window, and support contacts.	Keeps business teams informed and prepared.
Rollback Plan	Document steps to revert deployment if issues arise.	Provides a safe exit strategy in case of critical failure.

Post-deployment Validations

Area	Checklist Item	Why It Matters
Login and Access	Users can log in; role centers load correctly.	Confirms system availability.
Key Transactions	Post sample sales, purchase, and journal entries.	Verifies business-critical workflows.
Reports	Run Trial Balance, Aged Receivables/Payables, and Inventory Valuation.	Ensures reports reflect accurate balances.
Integrations	Refresh Power BI, test APIs, and check Outlook/Teams add-ins.	Confirms external tools remain connected.
Performance	Validate page load times and posting speed.	Detects bottlenecks early.
Approvals and Workflows	Submit and approve a transaction.	Confirms workflows trigger as expected.

(*continued*)

Area	Checklist Item	Why It Matters
Data Integrity	Spot check migrated records (customers, vendors, items).	Ensures data is complete and correct.
Audit and Logging	Confirm telemetry/logs are capturing events.	Helps monitor usage and troubleshoot errors.
User Feedback	Collect input from pilot users.	Identifies any gaps or pain points quickly.

Common Mistakes to Avoid

Mistake	Why It's Risky	How to Avoid
Skipping UAT	Leads to critical business processes failing in production.	Always complete UAT with business users.
No Backup Before Deployment	Makes rollback impossible if errors occur.	Take snapshot or backup of production.
Ignoring Permissions	Users may be blocked or gain excess access.	Review and test role permissions in sandbox.
Missing Communication	Users unaware of downtime or changes.	Send clear pre-deployment notices and post updates.
Deploying During Peak Hours	Increases risk of business disruption.	Schedule deployments in low-activity periods.
Overlooking Integrations	External apps (Power BI, CRM, payroll) may break.	Test and validate integrations in advance.
Not Documenting Changes	Makes troubleshooting difficult later.	Maintain deployment log with steps and versions.
No Rollback Plan	Delays recovery if critical issues appear.	Always prepare rollback instructions.

Case Study – End-to-End Business Scenario

Business Background

A mid-sized trading company in the wholesale distribution of electronic goods has been managing its operations through spreadsheets. This leads to frequent errors in stock counts, delays in invoicing, and a lack of financial visibility. The company decides to implement Microsoft Dynamics 365 Business Central (BC) to streamline its operations and integrate finance, sales, purchase, and inventory into a single platform.

Implementation Journey (Illustrative – 51 Days)

For the sake of illustration, this case study uses a **51-day project journey**. The goal is to show how functional and technical consultants collaborate step by step.

© Dr. Gomathi S 2025

Dr. Gomathi S, *Microsoft Dynamics 365 Business Central Essentials*, Apress Pocket Guides, https://doi.org/10.1007/979-8-8688-2229-2

Note   The 51-day timeline is an example, not a fixed standard. In real-world projects, the duration depends on project size, scope, customizations, and the number of users. Typical projects can take from **six to eight weeks for small implementations to several months for complex, multicountry rollouts.**

Implementation Journey
Phase 1: Requirement Gathering (Day 1–5)

- **Functional Consultant Role**

  - Meets finance, sales, and warehouse teams

  - Documents existing workflows and pain points

  - Prepares a **Fit-Gap analysis** to align business needs with BC features

- **Technical Consultant Role**

  - Validates whether identified gaps can be met using standard BC or require custom development

  - Assesses integration requirements with external systems (Power BI, Outlook)

Phase 2: System Setup (Day 6–10)

- **Functional Consultant Role**

  - Creates a chart of accounts and defines posting groups

  - Sets up dimensions (Region, Product Category)

  - Configures approval workflows for purchase invoices

- **Technical Consultant Role**

  - Prepares sandbox environment for testing

  - Creates templates for uploading customer, vendor, and item data

Phase 3: Data Migration and Configuration Testing (Day 11–20)

- **Functional Consultant Role**

  - Validates migrated master data (customers, vendors, items)

  - Tests purchase order and sales order postings for accuracy

- **Technical Consultant Role**

  - Executes **RapidStart packages** to import data from Excel

  - Troubleshoots migration errors (e.g., missing dimensions, incorrect balances)

Phase 4: Customization and Integration (Day 21–30)

- **Functional Consultant Role**

  - Defines scenarios where standard BC is not sufficient (e.g., warranty tracking)

  - Provides functional specs to developers

- **Technical Consultant Role**

  - Builds a **custom table for product warranty tracking**

  - Develops an extension for automatic credit limit checks in sales orders

  - Configures integration with

  - **Power BI** for sales and stock dashboards

  - **Outlook** for order entry from emails

Phase 5: User Training and UAT (Day 31–40)

- **Functional Consultant Role**

  - Prepares test cases covering finance, sales, and warehouse cycles

  - Conducts **User Acceptance Testing (UAT)** with end users

  - Guides staff in journal posting, purchase approvals, and sales invoicing

- **Technical Consultant Role**

  - Fixes bugs reported during UAT

  - Ensures smooth system performance

Phase 6: Final Preparations (Day 41–50)

- **Functional Consultant Role**

  - Validates closing balances and prepares cutover plan

  - Ensures business readiness for go-live

- **Technical Consultant Role**

  - Automates overdue invoice reminders using Power Automate

  - Finalizes deployment package for extensions

Phase 7: Go-Live (Day 51)

- **Functional Consultant Role**

  - Supports end users in real-time transactions

  - Monitors posting groups, financial reports, and user adoption

- **Technical Consultant Role**

  - Monitors system stability and integration flows

  - Resolves any post-go-live issues promptly

Outcome

- Sales and purchase cycles are fully automated.

- Finance team gains **real-time visibility** into receivables and payables.

- Inventory accuracy improves by 30%.

- Leadership uses **Power BI dashboards** for data-driven decisions.

- Manual effort is reduced significantly, leading to efficiency and growth.